HOW JUDGES DECIDE CASES:

READING, WRITING AND ANALYSING JUDGMENTS

"Whatever a judge does, he will most surely have his critics. If, in an effort to do justice, he appears to make new law, there will be cries that he is overweening and that he has rendered uncertain what had long been regarded as established legal principles. On the other hand, if he sticks to the old legal rules, an equally vocal body will charge him with being reactionary, a slave to precedent, and of failing to mould the law to changing social needs. He cannot win, and, if he is wise, he will not worry, even though at times he may ruefully reflect that those who should know better seem to have little appreciation of the difficulties of his vocation. He will just direct himself to the task of doing justice in each case as it comes along. No task could be nobler."

Lord Edmund-Davis
Judicial Activism
1975 (28) CLP 1 @ 13

"Proforma" Ideas - ref... 3.4 → p.63 {BASE OUTLINE}

HOW JUDGES DECIDE CASES:

READING, WRITING AND ANALYSING JUDGMENTS

Andrew Goodman LL.B., FCI.ARB.

Of the Inner Temple, Barrister
Professor of Conflict Management and Dispute
Resolution Studies, Rushmore University

To my wife, Sandra

Published by

xpl law
99 Hatfield Road
St Albans AL1 4JL
www.xplpublishing.com

ISBN 185811 331 8

Typeset by Saxon Graphics Ltd, Derby

Cover design by Jane Adams

Printed in Great Britain by Lighting Source

CONTENTS

PREFACE AND ACKNOWLEDGEMENTS

This is a work that is divided into very distinct parts. It is first concerned with the way in which modern judges, tribunal chairmen and arbitrators go about their decision making process as they compose their judgements, decisions and awards, and how they go about the task of delivering these, both at first instance and on appeal to the very highest level. It is then concerned with the mechanical process of how to read a judgement, a skill fundamental to the study and practice of law, and invites you to think in particular about why you should accept or reject what you are reading of the judge's findings and decision. You may be an experienced practitioner, or at the very outset of your career in the law; either way, I suggest and hope that there is something for each of you within these pages.

Next, I try to shed light upon the way in which judges compose their judgments. This involves an analysis of form, style, language and judicial reasoning. It looks at the way in which judges and tribunal members are trained in this area. When considering appellate jurisdiction, I stray into questions of collegiality, dissent and judicial law-making.

Finally I offer a word or two about problems with law reporting.

As I have made plain in my Introduction, much of this book was based on a study of the replies, kindly given by a substantial number of members of the judiciary, at every level, to a questionnaire that I prepared asking about their own approach to formulating and writing judgments. Their answers were provided on the basis that no attribution would be given to their personal views, and as such they provided a fascinating insight into the decision-making process, the pressure of time that judges work under, having to cater for more than one audience, their linguistic and literary skills, their training, the processes of formulating decisions in a tribunal consisting of more than one judge, the problem of dissent, and the procedure of the higher appellate courts. In trying to reduce this to a narrative I hope that I have captured something of the essence of the modern, business-like judge.

I have been greatly aided in this task by a large number of colleagues, professional acquaintances, and certainly some judges who gave very generously of their time, or permission to quote or reproduce their own writing on the subject. To that end I should like to thank in particular the following, and of course also express my gratitude to those who would prefer not to be recognised.

Jacqui Beech; HH Judge Christian Bevington; Master Bowles; Roger Bartlett; Zachary Bredemear; Rt. Hon. Lord Browne-Wilkinson; John Bryant; Rt. Hon. Lord Justice Chadwick; Simon Davenport; Nicholas Davidson QC; Robin de Wilde QC; Edward Faulks QC; Robert Francis QC; HH Judge Victor Hall; Alistair Hammerton; HH Rolf Hammerton; Veronica Hammerton; HH Judge Iain Hughes QC; Hon. Mr. Justice Jackson; Laura Johnson; Michel Kallipetis QC; HH Judge Marr-Johnson; Philip Naughton QC; John Norman; Sarah Paneth; David Pearl; Michael Pooles QC; Simon Readhead; HH Judge Roach; Louise Rones; HH Judge William Rose; John Ross QC; Mohinderpal Sethi; Martin Spencer QC; Andrew Warnock; HH Judge Welchmann; Master Whittaker; David Wilby QC.

Andrea Dowsett and the staff of the Judicial Studies Board; Brendan Keith, Principal Clerk of the Judicial Office, House of Lords; the staff of the Supreme Court Library; the staff of the Inner Temple Library; the staff of the Middle Temple Library.

And to my editors Catherine Cox and Andrew Griffin, many thanks.

I should make it plain that the opinions and polemic expressed in this work are entirely my own. I have borrowed some of the suggestions made from good practice that I have seen over the course of the last 26 years, which I both commend and hope will prove useful in this rapidly changing profession.

Andrew Goodman
1 Serjeants Inn
June, 2005.

TABLE OF CASES

INTRODUCTION

The idea for a practical book devoted to the deconstruction of judgments and judicial opinion came from a number of sources. First I discovered that the 1940 best seller *How to Read a Book*[1] by the renowned American education philosopher, Mortimer Adler, was still in print, and I recognised that the principles it contains are well suited to the study of judgments. Second, it seemed to me that the study of the process of making decisions, stimulated by Lord Bingham's essay *The Judge as Juror: The Judicial Determination of Factual Issues*[2] is itself worthy of wider examination. Third, upon inquiry, it appears that the kind of formal training in legal method which I enjoyed is no longer available on many law courses, particularly for CPE examinations. Fourth, my investigation into judicial training provided by the Judicial Studies Board suggests that, unlike certain tribunal chairmen, new Recorders receive fairly minimal training in judgment writing and presently, no formal appraisal.[3] And fifth, the government keeps hinting at the need to widen the base for judicial appointments: for both lawyers and litigants there is the frightening prospect of judges with little or no acquaintance with courtroom practice.

We are on the cusp of a new generation of lawyers who will have had no experience of contentious practice governed principally by domestic law under the direction of the Rules of the Supreme Court 1965 and the County Court Rules 1981: for them the doctrine of common law precedent is subject to both EU law and the intervention of the European Convention on Human Rights; the underlying philosophy of the Civil Procedure Rules 1998 means that settlement is preferable to and encouraged at the expense of judgment; the everyday use of ancient Latin maxims known to generations of lawyers and judges has begun to fade; and precise usage of the English language itself appears to be in decline. And if there is a new generation of lawyers, how far behind is the new generation of judges: already they are interventionist,

---

[1] Revised and updated in 1972 by Charles Van Doren (Touchstone/Simon & Schuster, New York) ISBN 0–671–21209–5.

[2] (1985) 38 CLP 1, reprinted in *The Business of Judging: Selected Essays and Speeches* Lord Bingham OUP 2000.

[3] A scheme is under consideration at the time of writing.

managerial and settlement minded. Indeed the imperative to force settlement in the face of a penalising costs regime could be said to emasculate, to an extent, the function of the civil judiciary.

In attempting to devise methods of reading and analysing judgments it quickly became apparent to me that I had to acquire an insight into how they came to be written, in terms of structure, language, style and content; and therefore to investigate how judges are trained both to come to their conclusions and formulate these, either orally or in writing; and how in fact they do so. Despite learned articles written principally by the well known legal philosophers of the last century, notably Professor H.L.A. Hart, Lord Devlin and, more recently Professors Ronald Dworkin and Basil Markesinis, the extent of practical literature in this area is very limited. I therefore determined that an empirical study was necessary in order to discover how judges go about their job.

To that end I have had the privilege of discussing their practical approach to writing judgments with members of the judiciary at every level, from Lords of Appeal in Ordinary, Lords Justices of Appeal, puisne judges of each division of the High Court and circuit judges of the County Court to recently appointed Recorders and full and part time Chairmen of various Tribunals, notably those dealing with employment and discrimination, immigration, transport and valuations, and with commercial arbitrators. The answers provided to my questions on the format, language, literary style, method of decision making, legal logic, concern over appeals, the problem of dissent and other matters – all integral to the creation of judgments – were given on the basis that they should not be attributable. This enabled judges to be candid, open, individualistic and enlightening, so much so that some of the information that I deal with in, for example, parts 2.4 and 2.8 I have never come across before in print, although often suspected when engaged in my practice.

What emerged was the difficulty in searching for a consistent approach, not so much as to report its existence, but to identify a suggested way forward to the next generation of both lawyers and judges. If this sounds presumptuous, particularly coming from one who holds no judicial appointment, it will be remembered that judgment and judicial opinion are important tools of the lawyer's trade, to rely and advise upon, to use to his client's advantage or save him from harm, as best he can. It is hoped, therefore, that this work will be of practical use to those considering the merits of an appeal, based on fair criticism of a judgment in hand; to newly appointed Recorders, deputy Masters or District Judges in considering how best to present their findings to the appropriate audience and at the appropriate level, and to students of that process.

What then, is the nature of judgment in our common law system at the beginning of the twenty-first century? It is a formal, authoritative, informed opinion having the force of law; the decision of an arbiter within a given juris-diction; the exercise of critical faculty, of discernment, discretion, good under-standing, and good sense in relation to two objects of thought or two conflicting arguments. In exercising judgment the judge's task is first to inform himself; then to make a reasoned decision; and then to inform others of his decision and reasoning. Once handed down the judgment is a matter of record and becomes conclusive proof of the claim so decided.

In writing or preparing a judgment, the judge caters for a diverse audience: the winning litigant; the losing litigant; the litigants' lawyers, family, friends, colleagues, supporters, shareholders, business associates, or competitors. His wider readership may extend to many classes of others – lawyers, law students, fellow judges, both of superior and inferior courts; foreign lawyers and practi-tioners, politicians, pressure groups, the media, and government.

The judge's principal objective is to make an effective, practical and workable decision. He is concerned with resolving conflict by determining the merits of conflicting cases, and by choosing between notions of justice, convenience, public policy, morality, analogy, and takes into account the opinions of other judges or writers.[4] In so doing he learns about the parties, and about their conduct in the particular circumstances; the trial is a living historical event that recreates the incident which is the subject of the litigation with the best evidence available. Each case therefore turns on its special circumstances, and the primacy of the facts is the key feature.

Cases in our courts are either won or lost in accordance with the requirement that the judge utilises the procedural code to act justly[5]. However the pursuit of justice for its own sake is an unrealistic abstract. The judge engages with real people and real conflict, where invariably he is faced with a choice between opposing parties, and has to do the best he can with the evidence available, according to the burden and standard of proof. This gives him an advantage over media commentators, over bureaucrats and public officials, and over legislators – he sits at the point at which the legal system makes its impact upon individuals and their lives. His reasoning and conclusion must therefore be practical, suit the facts as found, and provide an effective, workable remedy to the winner.

"COMMENTS ON SOCIAL CHANGE"

A frequent theme of this book is that modern judges are alive to the pressure and pace of social change, which seem to have intensified and accelerated over the past few decades. This is reflected in their confidence and willingness to bring the need for change into their decision-making process, whether from

---

[4] See Glanville Williams: *Learning the Law* 12th edn. A.H.Smith (Sweet & Maxwell 2002) 119,120.
[5] Civil Procedure Rules 1998 1.1(1): the overriding objective is for the court to deal with cases justly.

the House of Lords or at first instance. Perhaps the most stark example of this in modern practice was the removal in 1992 of marital exemption as a defence to the charge of rape. Lord Keith gave the leading speech in the House of Lords[6] and took the lead from the Scots approach:

> 'In *S. v. H.M. Advocate*, 1989 S.L.T. 469 the High Court of Justiciary in Scotland recently considered the supposed marital exemption in rape in that country. In two earlier cases, *H.M. Advocate v. Duffy*, 1983 S.L.T. 7 and *H.M. Advocate v. Paxton*, 1985 S.L.T. 96 it had been held by single judges that the exemption did not apply where the parties to the marriage were not cohabiting. The High Court held that the exemption, if it had ever been part of the law of Scotland, was no longer so. The principal authority for the exemption was to be found in *Hume on Crimes*, first published in 1797. The same statement appeared in each edition up to the fourth, by Bell, in 1844. At p. 306 of vol. 1 of that edition, dealing with art and part guilt of abduction and rape, it was said:
>
> > "This is true without exception even of the husband of the woman, who though he cannot himself commit a rape on his own wife, who has surrendered her person to him in that sort, may, however be accessory to that crime ... committed upon her by another."
>
> It seems likely that this pronouncement consciously followed Hale.
>
> The Lord Justice-General, Lord Emslie, who delivered the judgment of the court, expressed doubt whether Hume's view accurately represented the law of Scotland even at the time when it was expressed and continued, 1989 S.L.T. 469, 473:
>
> > "We say no more on this matter which was not the subject of debate before us, because we are satisfied that the Solicitor-General was well founded in his contention that whether or not the reason for the husband's immunity given by Hume was a good one in the 18th and early 19th centuries, it has since disappeared altogether. Whatever Hume meant to encompass in the concept of a wife's 'surrender of her person' to her husband 'in that sort' the concept is to be understood against the background of the status of women and the position of a married woman at the time when he wrote. Then, no doubt, a married woman could be said to have subjected herself to her husband's dominion in all

---

6 *R v R* [1992] 1 AC 599 HL @ 617F *et seq.*

things. She was required to obey him in all things. Leaving out of account the absence of rights of property, a wife's freedoms were virtually non-existent, and she had in particular no right whatever to interfere in her husband's control over the lives and upbringing of any children of the marriage.

"By the second half of the 20th century, however, the status of women, and the status of a married woman, in our law have changed quite dramatically. A husband and wife are now for all practical purposes equal partners in marriage and both husband and wife are tutors and curators of their children. A wife is not obliged to obey her husband in all things nor to suffer excessive sexual demands on the part of her husband. She may rely on such demands as evidence of unreasonable behaviour for the purposes of divorce. A live system of law will always have regard to changing circumstances to test the justification for any exception to the application of a general rule. Nowadays it cannot seriously be maintained that by marriage a wife submits herself irrevocably to sexual intercourse in all circumstances. It cannot be affirmed nowadays, whatever the position may have been in earlier centuries, that it is an incident of modern marriage that a wife consents to intercourse in all circumstances, including sexual intercourse obtained only by force. There is no doubt that a wife does not consent to assault upon her person and there is no plausible justification for saying today that she nevertheless is to be taken to consent to intercourse by assault. The modern cases *of H.M. Advocate* v. *Duffy*, 1983 S.L.T. 7 and *H.M. Advocate* v. *Paxton*, 1985 S.L.T. 96 show that any supposed implied consent to intercourse is not irrevocable, that separation may demonstrate that such consent has been withdrawn, and that in these circumstances a relevant charge of rape may lie against a husband. This development of the law since Hume's time immediately prompts the question: is revocation of a wife's implied consent to intercourse, which is revocable, only capable of being established by the act of separation? In our opinion the answer to that question must be no. Revocation of a consent which is revocable must depend on the circumstances. Where there is no separation this may be harder to prove but the critical question in any case must simply be whether or not consent has been withheld. The fiction of implied consent has no useful purpose to serve today in the law of rape in Scotland. The reason given by Hume for the husband's immunity from prosecution upon a charge of rape of his wife, if it ever was a good reason, no longer applies today. There is now, accordingly, no justification for the supposed immunity of a husband. Logically the only question is whether or not as matter of fact the wife consented to the acts complained of, and we affirm the decision of the trial judge that charge 2(b) is a relevant charge against the appellant to go to trial."

I consider the substance of that reasoning to be no less valid in England than in Scotland. On grounds of principle there is now no justification for the marital exemption in rape.'

The process of recognising and accepting change was summed up by Lord Hobhouse in *R. v. Governor of Brockhill Prison ex parte Evans (No.2)[2001] 2 AC 19 @ 48.*

"The common law develops as circumstances change and the balance of legal, social and economic needs changes. New concepts come into play; new statutes influence the non-statutory law. The strength of the common law is its ability to develop and evolve. All this carries with it the inevitable need to recognise that decisions may change. What was previously thought to be the law is open to challenge and review; if the challenge is successful, a new statement of the law will take the place of the old statement.

Two things follow from this. The first is that judicial decisions are not infallible or immutable. The doctrine of precedent recognises this and caters for it. Decisions of lower courts are not binding on higher courts. Even your Lordships' House[7] is able to depart from its previous decisions. Any decision is open to re-evaluation and reinterpretation. The second is that lawyers are well aware of this. They know that it is open to a client who is not satisfied with the existing state of the law to challenge it in litigation. This is done in a subtle way the whole time; only very occasionally will it be necessary or wise to do it head-on. But the choice is always there even though it will only be very rarely indeed that it is worth pursuing."

It is now widely recognised that from the latter part of the 20th century the common law judge began to participate in the incremental development of the law: he is a law developer as well as a dispute solver. This is to be seen at its most plainest in both applying the Human Rights Act 1998 to previous case law[8] and legislation,[9] in affording precedence to EU law over domestic

---

[7] (Ed.) after Practice Statement [1966] 1 WLR 1234.

[8] *R v Lambert [2001] UKHL 37; [2001] 3 All ER 577 @ [81]* and *Ghaidan v. Godin-Mendoza (FC) [2004] UKHL 30* per Lord Steyn @ [39] and Appendix C.

[9] e.g. *General Mediterranean Holdings v Patel [2000] 1 WLR 272 QBD; R v Secretary of State for the Home Department ex parte Anderson [2003] UKHL 46; [2002] 4 All ER 1049; R. v A. [2001] UKHL 25 @ [44]; Ghaidan v Godin-Mendoza (FC) [2004] UKHL 30;* and *D. v East Berkshire NHS Trust [2003] EWCA 1151; [2003] 4 All ER 796* per Lord Phillips MR @ [79-84].

law[10] and developing new remedies e.g. privacy[11] or extending the duty of care of professionals[12] or removing pre-existing advocates' immunity from suit.[13] The Commonwealth judge enjoys perhaps a greater role, with the higher Canadian and Australian judiciary increasingly confident in their ability to invade the domain of social policy, formerly the exclusive right of their respective legislatures.[14]

For good or ill unquestionably judges make new law, albeit fortuitously where the factual conflict which gives rise to litigation happens to give rise to issues of law for judicial determination.[15]

However it should be noted that courts have very little control over the pattern of law which later emerges from their decisions. The power of the higher courts to create binding standards is limited to cases which are closely similar factually; and in cases in which the decision is closely confined to the facts, no substantive law will be created.

Since no two cases are actually identical the judge can choose whether to be bound by a previous decision. His role is to conserve and uphold the existing law, and only infrequently to correct it. This flows from the fact that the right answer is always implicitly to be found in existing law, and judicial decisions are matters of principle tempered by what is fair and just according to the judge's personal moral, social and political standards:[16]

'Judicial decisions are, and should be, influenced by many factors...first, the judges' view of past law (statutes, precedents, and principles); second, the judges' evaluation of the consequences of the options before them; third, the judges' view of their own role...these factors are not always acknowledged by judges, who often prefer to squeeze them into the first issue...'[17]

In addition to the factors that influence his decision-making process, the judge must also consider the language in which he will give his decision. He will be concerned with the nature of his audience. Precisely to whom, among the many candidates, is his judgment primarily intended to speak? Has he

---

[10] *R v Secretary of State for Transport ex parte Factortame (No.2) [1991] 1 AC 601; Thoburn v Sunderland City Council [2002] EWHC 195; [2003] QB 151.*
[11] *Venables and Thompson v News Group Newspapers Ltd and others [2001] 2 All ER 908; Douglas and others v Hello! Ltd [2001] QB 967.*
[12] *X and ors (minors) v Bedfordshire CC [1995] 2 AC 633.*
[13] *Arthur J. Hall & Co. v Simons [2000] 3 WLR 543.*
[14] Mrs Justice Beverley McLachlin *The Role of Judges in Modern Commonwealth Society* (1994) 110 LQR 260.
[15] *The Common Law: Judicial Impartiality and Judge-Made Law* Prof. H.K. Lucke (1982) 98 LQR 29 @ 40.
[16] See Ronald Dworkin on Law as Integrity in *Taking Rights Seriously* (Duckworths 1977) and *Law's Empire* (Fontana 1986).
[17] *Judging Judges* Simon Lee (Faber and Faber 1989) p.201.

taken adequate account of contrary arguments within the framework of rational, ordered debate to enable him properly to decide where the legal right lies? Is the result pragmatic and purposeful? [18] Can he persuade his audience that his ruling is well-founded, correct and justified? If his judgment is to reach a wider audience, is it sufficiently accessible? He knows that uncertainty will breed further litigation. Is his decision to have only an immediate impact, in which case it can be couched in contemporary terms, or will it have some wider significance, and must therefore be able to speak to the future?

It is in this way that the common law has developed, with principles slowly established, altered, improved and refined by judges carrying out everyday functions. The parties receive their remedy; and the common law, as it exists in England and in jurisdictions strongly influenced by the English model, is judge-made in the sense that it is the by-product of the litigious process in the higher courts.[19]

This, therefore, is an attempt to discover the process of creating a judgment, which commences with an analysis of contested information and argument, moves on to reasoning and testing a possible solution, and so comes to a clear decision; and using a coherent and reasoned argument in a distinctive language, the solution is applied, so to emerge as law. It is written in the context of changing times for practising lawyers: important reforms in court procedure create a momentum which separates one body of the common law from that of earlier times.

Nothing could be truer of the introduction on 26th April, 1999 of the operation of the Civil Procedure Rules 1998.[20] Their teething troubles were a feature of some fun,[21] but now they have been in operation for a little while, only the likes of Franz Kafka are likely to be smiling, rather ruefully, at the judiciary. Now there is a ridiculous trend towards the courts being seen by government as merely a service industry with litigants as customers and the courts as service providers. The judges double as business managers, with an enormous extension of their discretionary powers, and a consequential increase in costs. Justice is no longer either an abstract or an ideal, but is a commodity qualified by proportionality, and subject to cost effectiveness. Fortunately, this work is not devoted to the Orwellian meaning of the words 'access to justice', but how such service is in fact provided.

---

[18] See *Advocates* David Pannick QC (Oxford 1992) p.10.
[19] *The Common Law: Judicial Impartiality and Judge-Made Law* ibid @ 33.
[20] To be read and given effect in a manner compatible with the rights and freedoms set out in the European Convention on Human Rights so far as it is possible to do so: s.3 Human Rights Act 1998.
[21] 'The junior members of my chambers tell me that the Woolf Rules impose three requirements on a judge – first, he must persuade people not to litigate at all; secondly, if that fails, send them to ADR; and if that too fails, strike them out.' Sir Christopher Staughton *What's Wrong With the Law in the Year 2000* Inner Temple Millennium Lecture, Inner Temple Hall 29 November 2000.

PART 1
HOW JUDGES DECIDE CASES

"The first principle of judging is dirty dogs don't win."
Lord Browne-Wilkinson

"Get the facts right and the law will look after itself."
HH Judge Hammerton

1.1
JUDICIAL TRANSPARENCY

In order to analyse judgments you need some insight into the decision making process of the judge. The single most important means of assessing whether you think a judge is right or wrong is to develop an understanding of how the judge has come to arrive at his conclusion, yet very little has been written by judges themselves about the practicalities of judgeship in modern times. The seminal work is an article written in 1985 by Lord Bingham entitled *The Judge as Juror: The Judicial Determination of Factual Issues*.[1]

That analysis of the common law judge's method of finding fact pre-dates both the Civil Procedure Rules and the adoption into British domestic law of the European Convention on Human Rights. The paucity of material on the subject of how judges decide cases suggests that, just as a particular judge's approach to writing a judgment is highly individualistic in terms of literary and linguistic style and format, so is his approach to decision-making.

Under Article 6 of the Convention all courts are now required under the Human Rights Act 1998 to give reasons for their rulings and judgments to demonstrate that a fair hearing has been conducted by an independent and impartial tribunal. In some courts this was already a familiar process, notably the Family Court and particularly after the implementation of the Children Act 1989; and in crime where courts were expected to provide reasons for refusing bail or imposing a custodial sentence.

The fact that reasons have to be given, usually in plain language so that a defendant to a criminal prosecution, or a litigant in person, can understand what has happened and why, demonstrates that the judge or bench has used a process of structured decision-making rather than reached a decision arbitrarily. This means that the losing party is more likely to accept the judgment

---

[1] (1985) 38 CLP 1–27, reproduced in *The Business of Judging. Selected Essays and Speeches* Lord Bingham (OUP 2000) which also contains a copy of his 1990 Royal Bank of Scotland lecture *The Discretion of the Judge* delivered at Oxford University on 17 May 1990, reported in [1990] *Denning Law Journal* 27.

of the court or tribunal, and if challenged on appeal, assists the appellate tribunal in supporting where possible the conclusion of the court below.

Academics and psychologists have long investigated decision-making techniques and further reading is available[2] on such scholarly topics as the theory of dynamic proof, the relationship between artificial intelligence or formal analysis and 'common sense', the logic of factual inference, including the relationship between causality and inference, the relationship between language and factual inference, the logic of discovery, including the role of abduction and serendipity in the process of investigation and proof of factual matters, and the relationship between decision and inference.

Our purposes, however, are practical. You are viewing critically the judge's ability to show the losing party and the Court of Appeal how he has arrived at his conclusions, the basis upon which he has resolved the key issues of fact, and why he assessed the witnesses in the way he has. The judge assesses the credibility and reliability of a body of evidence by asking how probable the account is in the light of agreed facts or any uncontentious background, of contemporary documents, and of the evidence of independent witnesses whose impartiality is not in question.

At the outset therefore, the judge must have in mind which facts are agreed and which are significantly in dispute if he is going to use the former as a benchmark against which to measure the latter. He must be able consciously to formulate a sufficiently detailed reason for preferring one witness to another. He has to consider, for example, whether it is essential to the decision that a witness is lying, or whether unreliability stems from honest but faded or distorted recollection.

---

[2] See various articles in LQR, MLR and CLP.

1.2
THE MECHANICS OF FACT FINDING

Most judges adopt the approach of first seeking out agreed facts as an anchor or base from which to build up a picture of what they can safely find is the more likely to have happened when forced to chose between conflicting events. If the likelihood is finely balanced and it is difficult to make a value judgment as to which evidence to prefer, they will rely on the burden of proof to come to a decision. If he who asserts a fact has to prove it, the task of the judge becomes far easier when deciding whether or not the standard of proof required has been met sufficient to discharge the burden.

Many judges admit to a fairly strong intuitive approach which develops with experience. They will fit the facts to a gut feeling of whether someone is lying, or of where the justice in the case rests. This can be limited to their analysis of specific material before them rather than the outcome of the whole case. Sometimes they use their intuition at the point where it becomes necessary to stand back and take in the whole picture; or where a key exchange in evidence becomes the centre of gravity of the entire case. In his opening remarks to a joint Chartered Institute of Arbitrators, Inns of Court and Bar Council lecture[3] in December, 1988 Sir John Donaldson MR, as he then was, stated:

> "It was always said of Lord Denning that he claimed to decide intuitively what should be the outcome of a case and then to go on to analyse the law in such a way as to justify his intuitive decision. Of course he was wrong to say that. Quite wrong. Most of us do exactly that, but we would not dream of saying so."

You must remember that for the vast majority of judges their sensitivity and reaction to witnesses comes from past experience as an advocate. The intuitive judge will say that the burden of proof method is rarely helpful although it

---

[3] *Judicial Techniques in Arbitration and Litigation*, Sir John Donaldson MR chairman.

can be determinative. It is more a question of stacking evidential beans as you go through the case, standing back and saying – does this result feel right?

Those who favour starting from an anchor point and then proceed to a logical development of the necessary findings in a case tend to establish a pattern of decision-making in which they decide each conflicting fact and apply law to it separately and then move on. This is a more generic approach since all of the available types of evidence are considered in relation to each factual conflict separately: thus a judge in relation to disputed fact 'A' will consider

- Is there contemporaneous documentary evidence available in respect of the issue the provenance and reliability of which is of assistance?

- Is there primary evidence of witnesses of fact?

- If so, is the documentary evidence consistent with the primary evidence of witnesses?

- If not, how to do the witnesses present: which is to be preferred?

- Is there secondary evidence available consistent with either real or primary evidence?

- If not, is there secondary evidence to which some weight may reasonably be attached?

- Is there evidence of system to which some weight may reasonably be attached?

- Is the intended finding on the issue consistent with undisputed findings or agreed facts?

- Is the intended finding consistent with a prior finding?

- Is the cumulative result correct?

Then the judge must move on to adopt the same process with disputed facts 'B' and 'C' and assess the position cumulatively.

It is reasonable to expect that the judge will have formed a general impression of the case from his preview of the papers. If he has time to read in properly he will note the opposing contentions in the primary evidence of facts and will consciously be looking for omissions, conflicts and ambiguities in the documentary evidence. This shows him the margin of dispute and materiality of evidence.

The fundamentals of viewing evidence will be ingrained: he knows, as do you, that the importance of direct or oral evidence of matters within a person's own knowledge is that it may be tested by cross-examination; hearsay evidence may not be tested and should be afforded lesser weight. Assertions of fact are not evidence unless admitted or supported by evidence. Inferences of fact may legitimately be drawn from primary findings of fact in certain circumstances, for example the absence without proper explanation of a document usually available to a party to prove a contested matter would create a legitimate adverse interest. Documentary evidence must be tested as to weight: whether in age, detail and accuracy the document is original and contemporary or whether it came into being for the purpose of the conflict; whether it is genuine, signed, dated, attributed, supports or detracts from oral testimony either in respect of the material issue, or another issue which might support or undermine its provenance. Above all, in evaluating the totality of the evidence relied upon by a party, the judge must ask – is it credible? Is it reliable? And where both sides are unreliable or there is nothing to choose between them, then he will apply the civil standard to the burden of proof.

Lord Denning considered that judges are seekers after the truth of what transpired,[4] although even if a judge expresses his judgment with confidence in what he finds happened, he can only do the best he can with the evidence available. Most judges who contributed to this book are not comfortable with a role that suggests they are seekers after truth. Whilst he must evaluate the reliability and credibility of oral evidence where he becomes involved in assessing conflicting accounts, the common law judge is not concerned with eliciting truth. The adversarial system means he merely has to decide whether, as between two opposing parties, the party who is advancing a claim has discharged the evidential and legal burden incumbent upon him if he is to win, that is, whether he has he proven case to the required degree of probability.[5]

The decision-making process is the culmination of a number of activities engaged in by the judge. He reads and hears the evidence; he chooses between the competing accounts of disputed events by preferring the evidence of one witness to that of another; he listens to legal argument; he considers the effect of previously decided cases; and he then decides who should win and who should lose.

As Lord Bingham puts it[6] the judge has to decide what happened, to piece together the story, and attempt, on the basis of all the available evidence produced in court, to reach a sound factual conclusion. It is obviously crucial to make positive findings of fact since almost all cases turn largely on the facts, and once found these are difficult to dislodge on appeal. He is faced with subjectivity, with chance, perjury, the risk of bias, the danger of false

---

[4] *Jones v National Coal Board* [1957] 2 QB 55 @ 63,64; but see *contra* Lord Denning MR in *Air Canada v Secretary of State for Trade* [1983] 2 AC 394 @ 411.
[5] The Business of Judging *op. cit.* p.4.
[6] *Ibid* p.1.

impression; the honest witness who may be frightened or irascible; the petti fogging witness who may be over scrupulous, may exaggerate or be garrulous, he receives the honest and convincing but mistaken witness; the witness whose evidence at best turns out to be his or her belief or opinion about someone else's belief or opinion; he has to make do with dead or missing witnesses, missing or destroyed documents; and he must cope with his own fallibility.[7] Lord Bingham's model for judicial fact finding can be summarised as follows:

1. Identify any common ground between parties. The statements of case or any concessions made in the skeleton argument should disclose this.
2. Resolve the issues of primary fact:
   (a) consider the unchallenged material;
   (b) weigh the force of contemporary documents, particularly those coming into existence prior to the dispute emerging, or any matters independent of human recollection.
3. Consider what happened against the background of independent material; against the same background consider what could not have happened.
4. Consider what *must* have happened *irrespective* of whether one or both parties say it did not.
5. Weigh dispassionately the merits of the opposing arguments.

A useful guide to the analysis of a witness's credibility was given in the speech of Lord Pearce in *Onassis* v *Vergottis*.[8] The points to be considered by judges are here set out in the form of questions it is suggested they should ask themselves:

- Is the witness a truthful or untruthful person?

- Is he, though a truthful person, telling less than the truth on this issue?

- Is he, though an untruthful person, telling the truth on this issue?

- Is he telling the truth as he sees it, i.e. has his memory registered events correctly?

- Is his memory subsequently influenced by unconscious bias or wishful thinking or by conversations with others?

- Has his memory become fainter or more imaginative with the passage of time?

---

[7] For a wider discussion see *Learning Legal Skills* Fox M. & Bell C. 3rd edn. Blackstone 1999 at pp. 99–100, 246–250, 256.
[8] [1968] 2 Lloyds Rep 403 @431

- What is the probability that he was mistaken?

- Is his evidence motivated by hope of gain, the desire to avert blame or criticism, or misplaced loyalty to one or other of the parties?

Lord Bingham also formulated the two additional tests to determine whether a witness is likely to be lying or not (where the judge is driven to conclude by reason of the nature of the case that he must distinguish between a witness whose evidence is merely unreliable and one who is being dishonest).

- Is the witness's evidence consistent with what is agreed or clearly shown by other evidence to have occurred?

- Is the evidence self-contradictory or otherwise inconsistent with a previous statement of the same witness?

Sometimes judges have to rely only on circumstantial evidence to establish what was the probability of an event occurring. Here the assessment of the evidence is more difficult than merely applying common sense. Even something very improbable may nonetheless have happened. Merely because the facts alleged seem bizarre, surprising or unprecedented by normal standards does not mean that such evidence should always be rejected. Having said that Lord Bingham takes the view that, "despite ... important disclaimers I think that in practice judges do attach enormous importance to the sheer likelihood or unlikelihood of an event having happened as a witness testifies in deciding whether to accept his account or not."[9]

---

[9] *Op. cit.* p.14

1.3

QUESTIONS OF WEIGHT IN FACT FINDING

Attaching weight to a piece of evidence that is the subject of conflict is essentially a balancing exercise. The judge must have regard to:

- the source and provenance of what he is being told;

- the circumstances in which the information came into being;

- how, when and under what circumstances the information came to be retained by the witness.

The credit of the witness in relation to a matter may not be germane to the litigation, and the court may derive no assistance from an unnecessary attack on credibility, in the sense that it has no direct application to the issue in question, unless it is concerned in truth with reliability. There are far more factors which give rise to unreliability than mere dissembling. These need to be considered separately:

- Does the evidence concern something occurring very quickly?

- Has the witness been exposed subsequently to misinformation concerning the event which might become absorbed into recollection; perhaps an unintentional distortion through contact with police, enquiry agents or solicitors?

- Has there been any loss of recollection over the passage of time – memory fades, and may fade selectively, not uniformly?

- Is the recollected evidence supported by contemporaneous notes; if so were these made independently or in conjunction with another witness?

- Has the witness engaged in subconscious wishful thinking through a process of exoneration or self-exoneration? Even experts may be partisan and lacking in objectivity where they fear criticism of their qualifications, experience, methodology or presentation.

- Has the witness 'improved' the evidence, fearing that the truth was too bare or unlikely?

When applying these questions the evidence emerges as separate pieces, each of different worth or value; it is not unlike a process of distillation or the sifting of items of value from among dross. And thus far we have been concerned only with primary evidence. Secondary facts (those inferences to be drawn from the primary material) need to be treated with even more caution. A good example is the weight to be attached to evidence of method or omission from method. A witness will say that he always does a particular act; the primary evidence shows or it is agreed that on the occasion in question the act was not done. Does the judge conclude that the act was not done on this particular occasion, or the evidence that the act was always done is unreliable? Does he accept method in preference to recollection, or does he confine such acceptance to circumstances where it can be used to corroborate direct testimony?

Whether it is proper to draw an inference from particular circumstances may be a matter of common sense to the judge, but his view of the position may be conditioned by his own background and experience. He may be drawing a conclusion that others would not. If the view he takes is one that others *could not* reasonably take, there will be grounds for an appeal. In training new magistrates the suggestion that common sense be applied to draw inferences from the conduct, demeanour and behaviour of defendants is now being withdrawn.

1.4
EVIDENCE ON OATH

Judges are not so unrealistic that they do not recognise a substantial proportion of the population displays a lack of respect for or otherwise merely pays lip service to swearing an oath to tell the truth. The religiosity of the nation generally, and the social values of many, have been steadily diminishing since Victorian times. On the other hand most lay witnesses do recognise the solemnity of the occasion, and understand that giving evidence is a serious experience outside the course of their everyday lives. Many are nervous on entering the witness box, and the proceedings operate to ensure that the whole of the court's attention is focused upon their oath taking. The procedure at that point is designed to make them feel exposed and self-conscious, and this is no bad thing for the administration of justice. If they are not overawed by the oath, it is at least to be hoped that witnesses understand the sanction for breach of it and the seriousness with which a judge will normally regard such a breach.

In a system that is adversarial a cynic might suggest in most cases, that one side or the other will probably be lying if only to exaggerate their position, and judges should be resigned to the fact that perjury is likely to be far more commonplace that we would choose to admit. Do people feel much sense of wrongdoing when they swear falsely if they can persuade themselves they are doing it in a good cause?[10] Probably not at the time, unless they are caught out. Yet both our system of justice and the position of the judge are dependent on treating as much of the evidence as possible as truthful, and the deponents as having been respectful of their oaths or affirmations. It may be something of a façade or a false hope in the early years of the 21st century, for people to be expected to be in fear of not telling the truth, yet the judge must take the promise of a witness at face value unless he is alerted by an inconsistency to believe otherwise.

---

[10] See *Evidence Proof and Probability* Sir Richard Eggleston QC (Weidenfeld and Nicolson 1978) p.159.

1.5

THE DILEMMA OF IMPRESSION

Ultimately the oral presentation of introduced evidence means that vital matters of judgment turn on impression. The demeanour of a witness may be of as much significance to the judge as the substance of his testimony. He has the advantage of watching closely the expression, the bearing, the delivery and the general manner of a witness. He will note the inflexion or vacillation in his voice. He will make eye contact.

Impression is also an important matter for appellate courts, in the sense that time and again the Court of Appeal has said[11] it will not interfere with findings of fact by a trial judge who has had the benefit of watching the behaviour and conduct of a witness, since hesitancy, the tone of voice or the nuance of an expression do not appear in the transcript, nor do blushes or the avoidance of eye contact. Inflections in both question and answer may be highly significant to the trial judge.

There is a problem, however. The impression given to the judge at first instance may be deceptive, and he should be wary of judging mainly by appearance. Lord Bingham makes the point[12] that a coherent, plausible, assured and well-presented story has always been the mark of a confidence trickster. For most witnesses the occasion on which they first come to give evidence is unnerving. They do feel very isolated and exposed in witness box, and to assess their credibility and reliability on demeanour alone would put the judge at a disadvantage. Hesitancy can be natural timidity or shyness but give the impression of being shifty. Looking down, rather than in the face when responding to a question, is seen in our homogeneous culture as a mark of evasiveness. Yet black youths are conditioned from birth not to look those in authority in the eye, to keep their eyes averted for fear of being thought insolent and disrespectful; to the British psyche this seems suspicious, cagey and unapologetic. The idea of giving positive consideration to cross-cultural patterns of communication in giving evidence, for example body language as

---

[11] E.g. *Onassis v Vergottis op. cit.* per Lord Pearce @ 431; *Clarke v Edinburgh Tramways* [1919] SC (HL) 35 per Lord Shaw @ 36.
[12] *Op. cit.* p.10.

well as tone of voice, is not a matter of political correctness. All judges will find the 1993 Kapila Fellowship Lecture given by the then Mr Justice Brooke on The Administration of Justice in a Multi-Cultural Society annexed to the Equal Treatment Bench Book, on the website of the Judicial Studies Board.[13] The examples of injustice he there describes owing to the unthinking behaviour of benches who fail to recognise the customs and culture of long established indigenous minorities make salutary, and fairly shocking, reading.

Many witnesses of other nationalities and other cultures pass through the court system daily: however even the finest judges have great difficulty in assessing the integrity of evidence given under interpretation.[14]

Witnesses who are honest and reliable concerning the substance of their evidence may well prevaricate about peripheral matters they may be asked about, particularly questions concerning their employment or the well-being of their marriage. Some witnesses are self-conscious in the face of an unwarranted intrusion on private matters, and this may well be reflected in the way they answer, giving an adverse impression. Of course it could be said that the whole purpose of cross-examination is to create an adverse impression in the mind of the judge, so that evidence in chief is not merely qualified but discredited.

One must also factor in the subjectivity of the judge: judges are still, deep down, human beings and creatures of their upbringing, education and experience. Inevitably they all hold different views and are subject to prejudices to varying degrees.[15] By and large we are extremely lucky in the selection of our judiciary: they are recruited not only for their intelligence and legal skills, reflected in the fairly small pool of successful practitioners from which they are drawn, but for both an innate sense of fairness and an appropriateness for the job as recognised by their peers. However their own value judgments will influence their decision-making in what they believe is or is not reasonable, and in particular this will shape the exercise of any discretion. That is why, despite media sneers, the work of the JSB's Equal Treatment Advisory Committee (ETAC) increasingly embraces broader concepts of equality, diversity, fairness and general 'judgecraft', in an attempt to achieve what is regarded objectively as best practice in administering justice for all.

---

[13] www.jsboard.co.uk.
[14] *Compania Naviera Martiartu of Blbao* v *Royal Exchange Assurance Corporation* (1922) 13 Lloyd's LR 83 per Scrutton LJ @ 97.
[15] Introduction to the JSB *Equal Treatment Bench Book 2004*.

1.6

DECISION MAKING IN INTERIM APPLICATIONS

Masters and District Judges are burdened by an enormous volume of applications, both procedural and substantive, and are therefore obliged to undertake relatively high speed decision-making, which is frequently no less important to the outcome of claims than decisions taken at trial itself. While much of their function is procedural, final awards made on interim applications, particularly summary disposal of cases, have no less force than judgments at trial. Despite concentrated hearing times Masters and District Judges must be able to formulate quickly a proper understanding of what the case is about. Pre-reading is likely to help them form a preliminary view.

Decisions made by judges working at this level are a combination of gut and brain reaction. They are partly based on common sense, and partly legal knowledge and experience. In the majority of cases experienced Masters and District Judges know what the answer is then build a logical case to explain it: they do not build a logical case to decide it. At the stage of an interim application in proceedings, even if one that delivers a final outcome, a relevant precedent, statute or rule, together with the principles for guidance set out in the Civil Procedure Rules, will carry the findings of fact in a particular direction to an obvious conclusion. If this leads to an obviously absurd, unfair or illogical result, that is usually an indication to the judge that is not the right answer, and he will revisit the position looking for a common base as his anchor, and then build a logical tower by progression. The latter is particularly the case where there is a litigant in person, and the Master or District Judge will often have to create from the argument of such a litigant a logical tower to see whether to accede to his position, or otherwise use it to explain why he must lose.

1.7

THE JUDICIAL DISCRETION

"An issue falls within a judge's discretion if, being governed by no rule of law, its resolution depends on the individual judge's assessment (within such boundaries as have been laid down) of what is fair and just to do in the particular case."[16]

The application of a discretion is one of the most important of judicial tools: in dealing with procedural applications, the grant of remedies and the award of costs the judge has what at first glance appears to be an almost unfettered discretion. It is the point at which he may choose between different courses of action, orders, penalties and remedies. Both before and during the trial the exercise of judicial discretion will determine applications concerning the statements of case, the admission of evidence, and the management of the trial itself. At its conclusion, after the findings of fact have been made, and after analysis of the law, it is employed when the judge has to decide what is the fair and just thing to do. It is the point at which the judge must exercise a choice in the course of action to be taken.

Fair criticism of a judgment will lead you to ask the question did the judge exercise his discretion properly? It is essential to be able to answer that question since appellate courts and tribunals will not ordinarily interfere with the legitimate exercise by a judge of his discretion. Case management decisions are also notoriously difficult to challenge. To mount a successful appeal you have to challenge the legitimacy with which the discretion was employed and so persuade the appellate body that no reasonable tribunal could have exercised the discretion in the way complained of.

Despite often being called 'unfettered', the exercise of judicial discretion is not a matter of a judge's personal whims and prejudices. In the procedural field what is regarded as the unfettered discretion of the master or district judge, particularly in case management, is still subject to authorities dealing with the way in which a particular discretion will usually be exercised, together with

---

[16] *The Discretion of the Judge* Lord Bingham [1990] *Denning Law Journal* 27.

the overriding objective and Article 6 rights. The guidance offered to judges by the higher courts, even under the Civil Procedure Rules, can be quite specific. Lord Denning MR provided a reason for this in *Ward v James*.[17]

> "It is an essential attribute of justice in a community that similar decisions should be given in similar cases. The only way of achieving this is for the courts to set out the considerations which should guide the judges in the normal exercise of their discretion. And that is what has been done in scores of cases where a discretion has been entrusted to the judges."

In the grant of remedies, particularly injunctions and orders for specific performance, the judge's discretion has been the subject of direction for well over a century:

> "The jurisdiction of the Court of Equity to enforce the specific performance, or to grant an injunction to prevent the breach of a covenant, is no doubt a discretionary jurisdiction, but I perfectly agree with the view expressed by your Lordships that the discretion is not one to be exercised according to the fancy of whoever is to exercise the jurisdiction of Equity, but is a discretion to be exercised according to the rules which have been established by a long series of decisions, and which are now settled to be the proper guide to judges in the Courts of Equity."
>
> *Per* Lord Blackburn in *Doherty v Allen*[18]

That is not to say that there should be a mechanistic application. The law requires a reasonable measure of consistency of approach, sufficient for you to consider whether the judge has acted in accordance with what would usually be expected in similar circumstances. If he has not done so, has he justified his departure and on what basis? This provides the beginning of a line of inquiry which might give rise to an appeal.

---

[17] [1966] 1 QB 273 @293.
[18] (1878) 3 App Cas 709 per @ 728.

1.8
DECISION-MAKING IN TRIBUNALS

By virtue of their composition, the tribunal decision-making process is a collegiate affair. The legally qualified chairman and lay members will have a preliminary discussion of the case, identifying the issues and taking the legal arguments from the written skeleton and oral submissions. The more experienced lay members will usually lead the discussion.

The way in which issues are considered critically is more mechanistic than the process used by a single judge. This is to enable lay members to participate fully in a sound and logical process where their decision-making can be both reasoned and justified. To that end the burden of proof become much more important as a yardstick against which to test the available evidence, and the JSB offers training[19] to tribunal members in:

- how to weigh evidence to assess what is needed to satisfy the burden of proof;

- how to evaluate the evidence necessary to resolve the conflict between opposing parties by not looking for absolute truth but preferring the evidence of one witness to another;

- the impact of oath-taking on credibility;

- the value of evidence being important, not the volume;

- the distinction between direct evidence and that requiring interpretation;

- practical guidance on the quality of evidence given, for example answers to open questions are likely to be of more value than closed questions.

---

[19] See *Weighing the Evidence* Mullan and Wilton, *Tribunals Journal* (2002) vol 9 No 2.

PART 2
THE APPELLATE JUDGMENT

THE APPELLATE JUDGMENT

Appellate courts and tribunals exercise supervisory jurisdiction, intended not only to review cases, but also to regulate and lay down the law comprehensively for the future. Even at the lowest level of appeal, though, appellate judges exhibit an in-built unwillingness to overturn a judgment or order of the court below unless it is demonstrably wrong. The starting point is that appeal courts wish to uphold judgments, particularly if there has been a clear exposition of the facts, law and reasoning by the judge below, unless they are forced, with reluctance, to do otherwise. This is nothing to do with judicial fraternity, although judges do have an inherent professional respect for each other. It is concerned with the primacy of facts. Judges deal with concrete facts and the application of law to those facts, not abstract legal ideas. The Court of Appeal wants to believe that the first instance judge has got it right, especially if adequate reasons are given for findings of fact. Very rarely is an appeal court ready to depart from a finding of fact or the exercise of a discretion by the trial judge. There is a real danger in doing so, since often judges sitting on appeal do not know the entire circumstances of the decision under scrutiny, even if they know the parts pertinent to the appeal. The Court of Appeal should not try to second-guess the trial judge; to do so regularly would be a recipe for chaos and inconsistency in the law.

In structure and language an appellate judgment will be different from that of the puisne judge. It will obviously be shorter on the facts and longer in its discussion and analysis of the relevant law. There is no element of the search for truth since the judge below has created a factual matrix which may only be undone in circumstances where no reasonable tribunal could have found such facts on the evidence available; or the even more unusual circumstance where relevant, probative evidence becomes available only after the trial and the appeal court is minded to admit it.

There must also be a measured approach to the language in which the trial or interlocutory tribunal is criticised. The Court of Appeal is very careful about criticising trial judges, since they are trying to do the job right, often under considerable pressure, and they undoubtedly do their best. Even muted criticism from a superior court causes pain and creates a different kind of pressure on the judge below. Harsh language is used very sparingly, and more often that not direct disapproval is understated, although its message is still conveyed.

2.1

DECISION-MAKING IN THE COURT OF APPEAL

By far the majority of appeals to the Court of Appeal are decided if not prior to the hearing, then certainly before its conclusion. This is not a matter of revelation, but pragmatism. The introduction of skeleton arguments has radically changed matters: judges are expected to read skeletons beforehand, are provided with reading days or other time in order to do so, and will form a view of the appeal prior to its commencement. There will usually be a pre-case discussion in which the preliminary view is aired between the members of the court and, if possible, agreed. Judges of the Court of Appeal also tend to talk to each other about the case at each break, even if only a few words. There are occasions when judges have an open mind on an issue to the extent that prior to the hearing they genuinely don't know the answer to a particular problem and need properly to evaluate the opposing submissions. Such occasions are in the fairly distinct minority; on ever fewer occasions will exquisite advocacy change a preliminary view, although it does also happen.[1] This renders the appeal hearing an exercise in the reality testing of a pre-existing view.

At the commencement of each appeal the judge presiding over the appeal will nominate a lead judgment writer. It is this judge who becomes the leading questioner of counsel. Since he must write the principal judgment he will formulate questions to assist him in the task. His judgment must also summarise the case and deal with the facts which were either found below or are agreed. He will also establish what points were found or conceded below, and those that were not canvassed and are being raised for the first time on appeal.

Since the Court will have read and absorbed the skeleton arguments of the parties the testing of a position is by question and argument:

---

[1] See, for example *Davies* v *Thompson* (op.cit.) per Carnwath LJ @ [55]: "I confess that I started the hearing of this appeal with a strong instinctive feeling that the claim should not be treated as time-barred....However, I have been persuaded by Miss Carr's careful analysis that this is the wrong approach."

"It is arguments that influence decisions rather than the reading of pages upon pages from judgments"

per Steyn LJ in *White v Jones*.2

The judge is best informed through a process of debate in which he will exercise his right to participate, and does so by asking probing questions. Appellate judges also have the opportunity to debate legal issues both among themselves and by using counsel as a foil. Senior judges favour the use of analogy, particularly in argument. If they do have preconceived ideas, and the hearing is an exercise to explore what is being advanced, analogy is useful in testing propositions, particularly by *reductio in absurdem*. This is often reflected in reported judicial intervention in submissions in the Law Reports, if not judgments themselves. Otherwise the Court of Appeal judgment uses the same literary and forensic techniques as first instance decisions: the text will contain questions and rhetorical questions, and be divided into units of writing for the convenience, and according to the personal style of the judge. Each prepares his own judgment, either dictated, which tends to make it longer and more conversational, or by word processor. Great care is taken with the use of language – in most cases over every word.

The key to decision making in the Court of Appeal is deciding the right question, or finding the right target. To do this a regular process can be discerned in judgments:

1. The Court starts with an overall understanding of the relevant law involved. This it often couched in terms of basic principle.
2. A close analysis is then made of the particular facts: ordinarily these are taken to be those found by the judge or which appear on the face of relevant documents, unless there is a particular reason for not doing so. The relevant facts must be identified in some detail.
3. The Court then asks itself what in the light of overall principle is the question which these facts require it to decide.

If this exercise is conducted, the problem then tends to solve itself. Usually there is sufficient guidance in the authorities on which side of the line these particular facts fall. The difficulty for the Court is where the facts as found or agreed are on the margin of the law. The Court will then look at the direction of recent law in this area, it being accepted that there is an ebb and flow to the pattern of decisions: if it can be identified which way recent decisions in the area are going, the facts may be applied to that law. Nourse LJ in *Stoke-on Trent Council v W. & J. Wass Ltd* gave an example of this approach:[2]

---

[2] [1993] 3 WLR 730 @ 751.
[3] [1988] 1 WLR 1406 @ 1415.

"...in a process of development it is sometimes necessary to stand back from the authorities and to ask not simply where they have come to, but where, if a further extension is made, they may go next. Although I would accept that there may be a logical difficulty in making a distinction between the present case and the way-leave cases, I think that if the user principle were to be applied here there would be an equal difficulty in distinguishing other cases of more common occurrence, particularly in nuisance. Suppose a case were a right to light or a right of way had been obstructed to the profit of the servient owner but at no loss to the dominant owner. It would be difficult, in the application of the user principle, to make a logical distinction between such an obstruction and the infringement of a right to hold a market. And yet the application of that principle to such cases would not only give a right to substantial damages where no loss had been suffered but would revolutionise the tort of nuisance by making it unnecessary to prove loss. Moreover, if the principle were to be applied in nuisance, why not in other torts where the defendant's wrong can work to his own profit, for example in defamation? As progenitors of the rule in trespass and some other areas, the way-leave cases have done good service. But just as their genus is peculiar, so ought their procreative powers to be exhausted."

When the system is working well, the question to be answered should be reduced to a form where it does not rely upon specialised knowledge. The usual constitution of the court is for there to be at least one judge from the discipline in question, although it is not unusual for the other judges outside the discipline to outnumber the specialist. The Court of Appeal undertakes a very wide area of work and often its approach in one area of the law makes good sense in another. Thus the particular area of specialisation is treated within an overview of the principles to be applied. To an extent this is reflected in the length of the respective judgments, since the specialist may wish to express his viewpoint on the law where otherwise a fairly short judgment might be called for.

In spite of what commentators may say about judge-made law, in the Court of Appeal there is in fact very limited scope for consciously making new law. The Court of Appeal needs to be a touchstone upon which both judges and practitioners may rely for consistency, and, to an extent, the conservatism of the law.

2.2

DISSENT

The curious feature of appellate judgments is the right and freedom to dissent. This flows from the individualistic ethos of the appeal court judges, and occasionally the tension between specialist and non-specialist opinion. At the highest level of appeal dissent may have a significant impact upon the weight and longevity of a decision, particularly in a developing area of the law. Dissent is not confined to the outcome of an appeal, since judges may be at considerable variance to the reasons for their conclusion, and may support a decision while expressly disagreeing with or qualifying a brother judge's analysis. As a precedent, a decision given 'of the court' has the substance of both collegiality and absence of dissent even as to particular reasoning.

In the Court of Appeal the pre-case discussion may indicate a lack of agreement by the members of the court. This is likely to be on one of the minority of occasions when either in terms of answering the question at hand the case may not be clear, or where at least two different views of the outcome can be taken. The presiding judge tends to persuade the others to the majority point of view in order to ensure unanimity. If such persuasion is ineffective, the judges will use counsel as a sounding board to get their points across or draw better points out of him. Advocates are encouraged to formulate arguments to assist the court. In this way the conflicting possibilities may be weighed against each other and a choice made between them. Competing arguments are indispensable to the judicial process, particularly at a level where it is intended to give guidance to the lower courts. At the conclusion of the appeal it will be obvious to the judges whether there is agreement or not.

Advocates tend to believe that dissent is noteworthy and closely watch both the composition of the court and look for the judge that appears to be the most supportive of their argument.

Dissent in reaching a conclusion on an appeal is still fairly rare, appearing in less than 10% of reported cases. There are some practical reasons for this. The dissenter will know that he has to write a judgment justifying his position. Some dissenters think there is very little point in providing a full dissenting judgment since it will not carry the day and unless they feel particularly strongly about an area of the law with which they are associated, it is some-thing of a waste of time. It may be worthwhile if they wish to address judges and practitioners in a specialist area, or there is a real prospect of the case going to a further appeal. The dissenter may be better off expressing his reser-vations outside the courtroom afterwards in the context of professional education or academic or legal literature. Lord Denning, who as Master of the Rolls found himself in the position of being a dissenter on more than one occasion, used his writing to justify his position. In *The Discipline of Law*[4] he devotes an entire section to his dissenting opinion in *Candler v Crane, Christmas & Co*[5] to make the point that, 14 years after it was delivered, the House of Lords finally approved it.[6]

Of course even the appointed lead judgment writer may be in the minority. If the lead judgment writer is the dissenter there will invariably be three reasoned judgments, at least two of which will be full. Even if it is in the minority conclusion, the leading judgment must provide a foundation for the others based on facts. The facts must be dealt with adequately to found a reasoned dissent.

FIND THIS BOOK

---

[4] Butterworths 1979.
[5] [1951] 2 KB 164.
[6] In *Hedley Byrne v Heller & Partners* [1964] AC 465.

2.3

THE APPEALS AND APPELLATE COMMITTEES OF THE HOUSE OF LORDS

The speeches and opinions of members of the Appeal and Appellate Committees of the House of Lords and Judicial Committee of the Privy Council are directed at the widest possible audience, to reflect their public interest and importance, since the absence of such criteria would render the subject matter unsuitable for consideration by the committees. A case is suitable to be argued before the House of Lords only if the issues involved are of general and public rather than of individual importance and must deal with questions of law rather than questions of fact. In criminal and courts-martial cases there is an additional, statutory requirement that permission to appeal cannot be granted either by the court below or by the House itself unless the court below has certified that a point of law of general public importance is involved in its decision.

When the appeal arrives, whether from the Court of Appeal or under the 'leapfrog' procedure from the High Court, the point of law at issue is formulated precisely in the form of a question. In 'leapfrog' appeals the High Court must certify that the case relates to the construction of a statute or statutory instrument or is a case in which the trial court and Court of Appeal are already bound by a previous decision of the House of Lords or Court of Appeal.[7] This approach allows the committee to focus its attention on, and formulate its opinion in respect of answering a specific question.

There are currently twelve Lords of Appeal in Ordinary. They are usually appointed from amongst the ranks of the Lords Justices of Appeal or, less frequently, judges of the High Court and they normally include two from the Scottish bench. Those engaged in drawn-out government inquiries diminish their number, and the Lord Chief Justice and Master of the Rolls sit as Appellate Committee members when required. In addition, former Lords of

---

[7] See further at *www.parliament.uk/documents/uploadHofLBpJUdicial.pdf.*

Appeal in Ordinary, former Lord Chancellors and holders of other high judicial office are entitled to sit as Law Lords under the Administration of Justice (Appeals) Act 1934. In practice few of them sit and then only occasionally. The composition of the committees is such that the most eminent and experienced judges discharge the judicial function of the House of Lords.

The Law Lords were constituted into an Appellate Committee in May, 1948. In 1960, authority was given for a second Appellate Committee to be appointed although it was not until October 1962 that two Appellate Committees sat for the first time concurrently. For the purpose of hearing appeals an Appellate Committee usually consists of five Lords of Appeal, though in cases of exceptional difficulty or importance the Committee may comprise seven members.

Appeals are normally heard in a public committee room, however at the end of the summer recess, before the parliamentary session has resumed, the Law Lords regularly hear appeals in the Chamber of the House itself, although this period is now limited by agreement to one week. The final judgment of an appeal is always given in the Chamber, usually on Thursday afternoons, by way of a vote upon the report of the Appellate Committee which heard the appeal in question. These sittings serve as a reminder that, despite modern practice, the theory remains that it is the Court of Parliament that hears and determines the appeals, and will do so until such time as a new Supreme Court is introduced as the final court for domestic appeals. For the same reason judgments of the House of Lords are referred to as speeches, and the decision in the appeal is put to a formal vote, consistent with the practice of all debates in the Upper Chamber.

If the court below grants permission to appeal to the House of Lords, the appeal proceeds direct to be considered by an Appellate Committee of the House. If the court below refuses permission to appeal, a party may seek permission from the House itself by presenting a petition for such permission within one month (14 days in criminal matters) from the making of the court's order. Every admissible petition is referred to an Appeal Committee (Standing Order 83 provides for two such Committees) consisting of three Lords of Appeal. The jurisdiction and present constitution of the Appeal Committee derive from the Administration of Justice (Appeals) Act 1934 and other legislation governing the bringing of appeals. Its chief function is to determine whether or not permission to appeal should be granted, though it occasionally still considers petitions on opposed incidental issues arising out of appeals and it is responsible for periodic amendment of the 'Practice Directions', which set out the practice of the House with regard to appeals.

The Appeal Committee considers the petition, which sets out the reasons for granting permission, together with relevant documentation. The Committee will decide whether permission should be refused or whether it should be provisionally allowed. If the Committee are unanimously of the view that a petition should be provisionally allowed the respondents to the petition are invited to submit objections within 14 days as to why permission should not be granted. Depending on the objections received, if any, the Committee will decide whether permission should be granted or refused, or, in cases in which the members of the Committee are not unanimous, the petition will be referred for a hearing. If no objections are received within the 14 days, permission is granted. In all cases in which the Committee are not unanimous the petition will be referred for a hearing. A public meeting of the Committee is held, attended by the parties, at which argument is heard. After the hearing the Committee decide whether leave should be granted or refused. Speeches given on these occasions are *ex tempore* and short. Reasons for refusal are given in accordance with the obligation of the Committee under Article 6.1 of the Human Rights Act 1998.

2.4

DELIVERY OF HOUSE OF LORDS' JUDGMENTS

Only in the most unusual and urgent circumstances do the members of the Appellate Committee announce their opinions at the conclusion of the substantive hearing. As the decisions of the House of Lords bind all the courts below, the Law Lords need time to formulate fully their opinions and their reasons for reaching them. Having arrived at their opinions, they are of no binding force until they are agreed to by the House. When the Law Lords' opinions are ready and have been printed, a sitting of the House is arranged, usually on a Thursday at 2.00 p.m., so that judgment may be given. Sittings for judgments, although only the Law Lords take part, are regarded as full meetings of the House. The presiding Law Lord sits as Speaker, the Mace lies on the Woolsack and a Bishop reads prayers after which the Principal Clerk of the Judicial Office, otherwise known as the Fourth Clerk at the Table, summons counsel and others to the Bar of the House and announces the consideration by the House of the report of the Appellate Committee in that appeal. The printed speeches are distributed just before the House meets and each Law Lord merely states that, for the reasons he has given in a speech which he has prepared and which is available in print, he would allow or dismiss the appeal. The House then delivers judgment by agreeing to the report from the Appellate Committee. The presiding Law Lord puts a number of questions from the Woolsack and they are agreed to or disagreed to on a vote. For example he may say:

> "The Questions is: That the Order appealed from ... be Reversed and the Order of Mr Justice...... be Restored. As many as are of that opinion will say 'Content', the contrary 'Not-content'."

Each of the judges having voted orally, the presiding Law Lord then announces that the Contents (or the Not-contents as the case may be) have it. After any further questions that may be necessary, for example on costs, have been put and voted upon, the Clerk calls, "Clear the Bar". After the House has given its judgment the Judicial Office draws up a written order signed by the Clerk of the Parliaments as Registrar of the court. Since

November 1996, House of Lords Judgments have been available on the Internet within 2 hours of delivery. They can be found, among other places, at *www.parliament.uk.*

2.5
DECISION MAKING BY THE APPELLATE COMMITTEE

At the conclusion of argument on the substantive hearing of an appeal, the Appellate Committee meets in private to discuss and review the case, and for each member to express his or her initial opinion, however firm or tentative. The process is informal, save that the most junior Law Lord is required to express his or her view first. This procedure underlines the independence of each member of the Committee, since it eliminates the possibility of a more senior or forceful judge expressing an opinion with which a junior or inexperienced member might be uncomfortable in disagreeing. Such discussions may be short or lengthy depending upon each appeal. There are no hard and fast rules, and the proceedings are flexible to the extent that a casual observer might think them to be *sui generis*. There is no designated lead opinion writer, however the presiding judge will usually ask one member to be responsible for outlining the facts, and another to deal with the relevant legislative antecedents or the historical development of precedent in respect of the questions posed.

A striking feature of this court is that each judge operates entirely independently, undertaking his or her own research with the help of judicial assistants, and forming an individual view. This is reflected in the personal style of judgments and the favoured items of influence. For example Lord Steyn favours academic treatises and both he and Lord Goff the use of international comparative law. The use made in judicial opinion of academic literature or foreign law is not recent.[8]

There is no pressure in terms of time, unless it is agreed during the hearing that the matter has a particular urgency: the fact that a large number of decisions in lower courts are being held in suspended animation to abide the outcome of a particular appeal, or conjoined appeals concerning similar subject matter, does not operate to speed up the process. The judges must be

---

[8] See *Rowling* v *Takaro Properties Ltd* [1988] 1 AC 473 @ 500 per Lord Keith; *Derbyshire County Council* v *Times Newspapers* [1993] AC 534.

afforded as much time as they need to feel satisfied with the correctness and workability of an opinion which will determine the law and bind the courts for some time in the future. This period of reflection allows members of the Committee even to change their minds: see, for example Lord Millett in *Wadey v Surrey County Council [2000] 1 WLR 820* at 840 C-F.

Neither is there any pressure or influence brought to bear by the more senior members. A Lord of Appeal in Ordinary may write as much or as little in his or her opinion as they wish.

One judge who has particular views or a particular interest in the subject matter of the appeal may take a lead and circulate his draft opinion to his brethren. This may influence the other members of the Committee, particularly if it both accords with their general view of the matter and they have yet to start work on a substantive opinion of their own. Reports containing only one principal reasoned judgment suggest where this is likely to have happened.[9] It may also be the case that the views expressed in the meeting at the conclusion of the hearing are tentative and open to persuasion on further consideration. Members of the Committee may and do meet informally to discuss the progress of own opinions.

It is unlikely that this flexible and practical approach will be changed by the removal of the Law Lords into a proposed Supreme Court of final domestic appeal.

---

[9] For example the speech of Lord Hoffmann in *South Australia Asset Management Co. Ltd v York Montague [1997] AC 191.*

2.6

THE APPELLATE COMMITTEE AND JUDGE-MADE LAW

WHO decided that corp m/sl = GNM? WHY?? BASED

If law is the articulation of a standard, whether of social conduct, proprietary or personal rights, duties or remedies, the role of precedent is to take that standard and project it into the future as a binding rule.[10] The role of the superior courts is to superintend the operation of the law, ensure that it is coherent, works in practice, and is accessible at least to those who regulate and practice it, if not to those who are affected by its operation. The House of Lords, being at the apex of our system of precedent, will modify legal rules and standards as necessary to suit the public interest requirement that the law should meet changes in contemporary social and economic values and be workable in that context.

There appear to be two general principles at work which drive the policy considerations of the Appellate Committees. First, there is a general reluctance to overrule precedent unless it is plainly no longer workable: a precedent really needs either to be *per incuriam*, or out with the modern workings of society. Lord Lowry considered this in *C (A Minor) v DPP*[11] when the House of Lords was considering whether the principle of *doli incapax* was still good law in England and Wales:

> "In *Reg. v Knuller (Publishing, Printing and Promotions) Ltd.* [1973] A.C. 435 Lord Simon of Glaisdale made two points which are most relevant to the present appeal. He observed, at p. 489C, that the House was concerned with highly controversial issues on which there was every sign that neither public nor parliamentary opinion was settled. Then, at p. 489E, he said that Parliament had had several opportunities to amend the law but had not taken them. He quoted the words used by Lord Reid in *Shaw v Director of Public Prosecutions* [1962] A.C. 220, 275, when he said: "Where Parliament fears to tread it is not for the courts to rush in.""

---

[10] *The Common Law: Judicial impartiality and Judge-Made Law* Prof. H.K. Lücke [1982] 98 LQR 29 @ 45.
[11] [1996] AC 1 @ 28.

FIND?

Again, Lord Simon in *Director of Public Prosecutions for Northe*
v *Lynch* [1975] A.C. 653, 696A referred to "matters of social
which the collective wisdom of Parliament is better suited t(

In my dissenting speech in *Reg.* v *Gotts* [1992] 2 A.C. 412, in which by
a majority your Lordships held that a plea of duress was of no avail in
defence to a charge of attempted murder, I drew attention, at p. 440,
to two statements contrasting the functions of Parliament and the
judges. In *Abbott* v *The Queen* [1977] A.C. 755 Lord Salmon said, at p.
767:

ON THESE POINTS

"Judges have no power to create new criminal offences; nor in their
Lordships' opinion, for the reasons already stated, have they the
power to invent a new defence to murder which is entirely contrary to
fundamental legal doctrine accepted for hundreds of years without
question. If a policy change of such a fundamental nature were to be
made it could, in their Lordships' view, be made only by Parliament.
Whilst their Lordships strongly uphold the right and indeed the duty
of the judges to adapt and develop the principles of the common law
in an orderly fashion they are equally opposed to any usurpation by
the courts of the functions of Parliament."

And in *Reg.* v *Howe* [1987] A.C. 417 Lord Mackay of Clashfern,
speaking of judicial legislation said, at pp. 449–450:

"In approaching this matter, I look for guidance to Lord Reid's
approach to the question of this House making a change in the
prevailing view of the law in *Myers* v *Director of Public Prosecutions*
[1965] A.C. 1001, 1021–1022, where he said: 'I have never taken a
narrow view of the functions of this House as an appellate tribunal.
The common law must be developed to meet changing economic
conditions and habits of thought, and I would not be deterred by
expressions of opinion in this House in old cases. But there are limits
to what we can or should do. If we are to extend the law it must be by
the development and application of fundamental principles. We
cannot introduce arbitrary conditions or limitations: that must be left
to legislation. And if we do in effect change the law, *we ought in my
opinion only to do that in cases where our decision will produce some
finality or certainty.*'" (Emphasis supplied.)

It is hard, when discussing the propriety of judicial law-making, to
reason conclusively from one situation to another, but a further
example of reluctance to interfere with a fundamental doctrine, the
rule against hearsay, is provided by the difficult case of *Reg.* v *Kearley*
[1992] 2 A.C. 228 decided in your Lordships' House. I refer to the

statements of my noble and learned friends, Lord Bridge of Harwich, at p. 251, and Lord Ackner, at p. 258, and of Lord Oliver of Aylmerton, at pp. 277–278. I believe, however, that one can find in the authorities some aids to navigation across an uncertainly charted sea. (1) If the solution is doubtful, the judges should beware of imposing their own remedy. (2) Caution should prevail if Parliament has rejected opportunities of clearing up a known difficulty or has legislated, while leaving the difficulty untouched. (3) Disputed matters of social policy are less suitable areas for judicial intervention than purely legal problems. (4) Fundamental legal doctrines should not be lightly set aside. (5) Judges should not make a change unless they can achieve finality and certainty. I consider that all these aids, in varying degrees, point away from the solution proposed in the court below.'

Secondly, the Committee will not be shy of moving tentatively in a new direction if that is what justice requires, or as Lord Goff described it in *White v Jones, 'the impulse to do practical justice'*.[12] This can, of course, lead to extreme, and some would say quite extraordinary results, as appears to have been the case in *Fairchild v Glenhaven Funeral Services Ltd [2003] 1 AC 32* where the Committee, on any orthodox view, appear to have suspended the law of causation in its entirety, since "any other outcome would be deeply offensive to instinctive notions of what justice requires and fairness demands.[13]"

That any movement can be described as tentative even when creating a new precedent, reflects the primacy of the facts, even at the level of the highest court of appeal. The Law Lords are no less interested in and constrained by the facts of the case than any of their brethren in the courts below. However rarefied and abstruse the legal argument before the Committee, it must be anchored in the facts of the case: while the judges will feel free to expound upon the most general of principles in order to provide guidance for the future, the actual decision on the appeal will turn on the facts, even if the detail of the argument is quite remote from them.

Traditionally the Law Lords have expressed in strong terms the view that judges should be reluctant to bring about far reaching changes in law: see, for example, the speech of Lord Reid in *Suisse Atlantique Société d'Armement Maritime S.A. v N.V. Rotterdamsche Kolen Centrale.*[14]

"If this new rule of law is to be adopted, how far does it go? In its simplest form it would be that a party is not permitted to contract out of common law liability for a fundamental breach. If that were right

---

[12] *[1995] 2 AC 207 @ 259G*
[13] per Lord Nicholls of Birkenhead @36
[14] *[1967] 1 AC 367 @ 405.*

then a demurrage clause could not stand as limiting liability for loss resulting from a fundamental breach: and the same would apply to any clause providing for liquidated damages. I do not suppose that anyone has intended that this rule should go quite so far as that. But I would find it difficult to say just where the line would have to be drawn.

In my view no such rule of law ought to be adopted. I do not take that view merely because any such rule is new or because it goes beyond what can be done by developing or adapting existing principles. Courts have often introduced new rules when, in their view, they were required by public policy. In former times when Parliament seldom amended the common law, that could hardly have been avoided. And there are recent examples although, for reasons which I gave in *Shaw v. Director of Public Prosecutions,* I think that this power ought now to be used sparingly. But my main reason is that this rule would not be a satisfactory solution of the problem which undoubtedly exists."

and that of Lord Fraser in *Hesperides Hotels* v *Aegean Turkish Holidays:*[15]

"If the matter were free from authority, there would be much to be said for what Mr. Kemp suggested was the true rule to be extracted from the *Moçambique* case, videlicet that the English court has jurisdiction to entertain an action for damages for trespass to foreign land against a person within the jurisdiction in a case where title is not in dispute and where there is no real dispute as to the plaintiff's right to possession of the land. But the matter is not free from authority and, in my opinion, this is not one on which it would be right for the House to depart from its earlier decisions. The main reason is that I do not think that the House in its judicial capacity has enough information to enable it to see the possible repercussions of making the suggested change in the law. One probable repercussion would be that, if the English courts were to have the wider jurisdiction of the suggested "true rule," they might at the same time have to limit their new jurisdiction by applying to it a rule of forum non conveniens. Since *The Atlantic Star* [1974] A.C. 436 and *MacShannon* v *Rockware Glass Ltd.* [1978] A.C. 795, this might not be a revolutionary step, but it would nevertheless represent a consequential change in the law of some significance. There may well be other and more important repercussions. I would apply to this question the words of my noble and learned friend, Lord Simon of Glaisdale, in *Miliangos* v *George Frank (Textiles) Ltd.* [1976] A.C. 443, 480:

---

[15] [1979] AC 508 @ 544.

"I do not think that this is a 'law reform' which should or can properly be imposed by judges; it is, on the contrary, essentially a decision which demands a far wider range of review than is available to courts following our traditional and valuable adversary system – the sort of review compassed by an inter-departmental committee." "

This approach was put very well in the Australian case of *SGIC* v *Trigwell* (1979) 26 ALR 67 @ 78 per Mason J:

"I do not doubt that there are some cases in which an ultimate court of appeal can and should vary or modify what has been thought to be a settled rule or principle of the common law on the ground that it is ill-adapted to modern circumstances. If it should emerge that a specific common law rule was based on the existence of particular conditions or circumstances, whether social or economic, and that they have undergone a radical change, then in a simple or clear case the court may be justified in moulding the rule to meet the new conditions and circumstances. But there are very powerful reasons why the court should be reluctant to engage in such an exercise. The court is neither a legislature nor a law reform agency. Its responsibility is to decide cases by applying the law to the facts as found. The court's facilities, techniques and procedures are adapted to that responsi-bility; they are not adapted to legislative functions or to law reform activities. The court does not, and cannot, carry out investigations or inquiries with a view to ascertaining whether particular common law rules are working well, whether they are adjusted to the needs of the community and whether they command popular assent. Nor can the court call for, and examine, submissions from groups and individuals who may be vitally interested in the making of changes to the law. In short, the court cannot, and does not, engage in the wide-ranging inquiries and assessments which are made by governments and law reform agencies as a desirable, if not essential, preliminary to the enactment of legislation by an elected legislature".

The House may wish to express clear views about the state of social mores in terms of perceived changes in popular values concerning, for example, sexual behaviour (as in *R* v *R* [16]) but is still conservative in its approach to policy while acting as guardians of our morality: see *R* v *Brown*.[17]

Judge-made law is still the subject of considerable debate, and in the eyes of some distinguished judges remains wrong in principle. With his typically

---

[16] [1992] 1 AC 599.
[17] [1993] 2 All ER 75 HL.

acerbic wit, Sir Christopher Staughton gave two good examples in his Inner Temple Millennium Lecture:[18]

> "*R. v R.*[19] ...is one of the two cases which to my mind demonstrate when the judges should *not* make new law. I do not see how it can properly be described as an extension. It changed what was substantive law established for a very long time. Its retrospective operation would seem to be in breach of the Convention,[20] Article 7, which I have already quoted. But of course we have to remember that the Convention, like other European legislation, only means what it says when the result conforms with the supposed intention of the legislator. Otherwise it means something different.
>
> I hold no brief for rapacious husbands, you will be glad to hear. But the decision of the Court of Appeal[21] in that case was a clear example of inappropriate legislation by judges. Why did Parliament not alter the law about matrimonial rape? It would have required very little of the Members' time, I suppose. And as to the political effect, the reform would no doubt have attracted rather more votes from women than opposition from men. But Parliament did not do it.

> My second example is the recent decision of the House of Lords in *Arthur Hall & Co v Simons,*[22] which abolished the immunity of advocates in civil, and by a majority of four to three, in criminal cases. A striking feature of the case was that Parliament had expressly recognised, as it seems to me, the immunity of advocates in section 62 of the Courts and Legal Services Act 1990. As Lord Hope of Craighead said, "attempts were made in both Houses to abolish the immunity, but proposed amendments to that effect were withdrawn after debate." So this was not a case where Members of Parliament were short of time. But Lord Hope added: "the fact that Parliament has not seen fit to abolish the case for immunity" (I would say declined to abolish it) "does not, of course, mean that your Lordships should feel inhibited from taking that initiative". Lord Hobhouse put it even higher than that. He said : "Parliament ...has implicitly left it to the Courts to consider whether the immunity should survive." I do not think that Parliament did anything of the kind.

---

[18] *What's Wrong With the Law in the Year 2000* Inner Temple Hall 29 November 2000.
[19] [1992] 1 AC 599 pr Lord Lane LCJ @ 603B et seq in which the Court of Appeal held that a husband may be guilty of the rape of his wife.
[20] European Convention on Human Rights.
[21] This was upheld in the House of Lords: [1992] 1 AC 599 @614 *et seq.*
[22] [2000] 3 WLR 543.

Once again, I have no brief to argue for the immunity of advocates, be it good or bad. But we have the situation that a substantive rule of law which, as Lord Steyn said, had existed in the case of barristers for more than two centuries, had been abolished by the votes of seven Lords of Appeal in Ordinary when Parliament had expressly declined to change it. What is more, the rule for criminal cases was abolished only by a majority of four to three. A populist analysis, which of course I do not adopt, would be that it was abolished by Lord Millett alone."

Though humorous in vein, Sir Christopher makes a telling point about the operation of dissent in the House of Lords. He is really suggesting that such freedom devalues the weight of a decision which nonetheless binds all other courts, and, subject to the ability not to follow its own decisions, those dissenting members of the Appellate Committee of the House themselves.

The student of the mechanics of dissent at the highest level would do well to consider the approach of the members of the Appellate Committee in *R. v Kansal (No.2)*[23] after the dissenting opinion of Lord Steyn in *R. v Lambert*[24] and also that of Lord Hoffmann in the Judicial Committee of the Privy Council in *Lewis v Attorney General of Jamaica.*[25]

In his analysis[26] of the decisions of *Lewis, Lambert* and *Kansal (No.2)* the distinguished New Zealand academic, Professor B. V. Harris, devised an inventory of those considerations relevant to a final court of appeal in deciding whether to defer to or overrule existing court of final appal precedent. This has a wider application, since many (though not all) of these same factors will assist you in examining whether any judge has properly applied, or conversely not followed, a particular precedent (see Part 5.10):

- Can it be distinguished on either the facts, the social context or the law at the time it was made? If so there is no need for the court to overrule a case which can be distinguished.

- Was the precedent decided *per incuriam*, specifically having failed to consider a relevant authority from a superior court of record or a piece of relevant legislation? If so it can be overruled.

- Is the precedent still workable in the context of contemporary standards, values and practices? If so it should be followed, if otherwise, not followed.

---

[23] [2001] UKHL 62; [2001] 3 WLR 1562.
[24] [2001] UKHL 37; [2001] 3 WLR 206 per Lord Steyn @ 213.
[25] [2001] 2 AC 50 per Lord Hoffmann @ 87.
[26] *Final Appellate Courts Overruling Their Own 'Wrong' Precedents: The Ongoing Search for Principle* Prof. B V Harris (2002) 118 LQR 408 @ 422.

- Has any argument been advanced on appeal which was not considered in deciding the precedent? If so it need not be followed.

- Does the later court continue to regard the precedent as wrong, notwithstanding that none of the foregoing apply? If so the court requires an alternative path of reasoning – it may give a different weight or priority to the reasons taken into account in precedent. If it can do so it may properly justify not following the precedent.

- Taking the weight of the precedent into account, how may the court meet the need to arrive at what each judge considers to be the most just resolution of conflict?

- What is the likelihood of the legislature overruling the precedent which is considered wrong?

- Does the litigation involve an issue of fundamental principle e.g human or civil rights? If so the Court should be more inclined to overrule a precedent that will enable it to do justice by principles fundamental to society.

2.7

JUDICIAL COMMITTEE OF THE PRIVY COUNCIL

The Judicial Committee of the Privy Council is the court of final appeal for the United Kingdom's overseas territories and Crown dependencies, and for those Commonwealth countries that have retained the appeal to Her Majesty in Council or, in the case of Republics, to the Judicial Committee with the Queen nominally the hearer of the petition. It is also the court of final appeal for determining "devolution issues" under the United Kingdom devolution statutes of 1998 and it has certain other domestic jurisdiction within the United Kingdom, hearing appeals from the Channel islands, ecclesiastical authorities and dealing as a review body for decisions of the disciplinary panels of various professional bodies, such as the Royal College of Veterinary Surgeons.

Members of the Judicial Committee include the Lord Chancellor and past Lord Chancellors; the Lords of Appeal in Ordinary, who, together with past and present members of the Courts of Appeal of England and Wales and Northern Ireland and of the Inner House of the Court of Session in Scotland do most of the judicial work; other Lords of Appeal, including former Lords of Appeal in Ordinary; other Privy Councillors who hold or have held high judicial office (i.e. are or have been judges of superior courts) within the United Kingdom; and Privy Councillors who are judges of certain superior courts in other Commonwealth countries: at present there are 15 of these overseas members.

Five judges normally sit to hear Commonwealth and devolution appeals and three for other matters, although in matters of very significant importance a panel of seven or even nine may be constituted. The Judicial Committee deals with about 55–65 Commonwealth and devolution appeals a year, and sits in the Privy Council Chamber in Downing Street. Since the statutory jurisdiction of each type of appeal regulates them separately one can only say that, broadly speaking, proceedings are conducted in a similar way to the Appeals Committee in the Lords with appeals being brought only with leave either of the court appealed from or by special leave of the Judicial Committee. Special leave will only be granted if the case raises a far-reaching question of law or a matter of dominant public importance. The proceedings are regulated by the Judicial Committee (General Appellate Jurisdiction) Rules 1982[27] and practice directions issued by the Registrar of the Privy Council.

The hearing of the petition for leave is usually of between 20 and 30 minutes duration with the advocates making their submissions before the table around which the judges sit unrobed. At the conclusion of argument the advocates retire for the judges to deliberate after which they are asked to return. The decision is announced *ex tempore* in the form that a report will be submitted to Her Majesty in Council advising that the petition be dismissed or that it be heard. Reasons for the decision are generally not given.

At the conclusion of argument on the substantive hearing of an appeal, the Judicial Committee ordinarily reserves judgment and then meets in private to discuss and review the case, and, much as the Appellate Committee in the House of Lords, for each member to express his or her initial opinion, however firm or tentative. The process is again very informal and under the procedural guidance of the Registrar, the proceedings are very much *sui generis*.

At the delivery of judgment the result of the appeal is announced in open court although the reasons are not given or read out. These will have been produced and distributed to the parties and any other appropriate person before the hearing for judgment. The form of the judgment is a report to Her Majesty advising her as to the outcome of the appeal. The report is then formally submitted to the Queen for her approval to be embodied as an Order in Council at the next meeting of the Council.

The report to the Queen provided by the Judicial Committee is traditionally in the form of a single opinion of the court advising whether the appeal should be allowed or dismissed. However since 1966[28] members of the Committee have been able to publish a dissenting opinion. It is still the case that by far the majority of decisions of the Judicial Committee are collegial, but there has been an increase in dissenting opinions over recent years, particularly in cases of significant jurisprudential difficulty or those having a wide impact on the law of the recipient state or authority.

---

[27] SI 1982/1676.
[28] Judicial Committee (Dissenting Opinions) Order 1966 (4th March 1966).

PART THREE
READING JUDGMENTS

3.1

SOME BASIC PRINCIPLES: FOCUS AND TIME

With respect to the many fine members of law faculties and departments across the country, law is not a subject that is readily taught. Unlike purer academic subjects it is not easily accessible. To understand law involves a process of learning by individual self-discovery – of research, of investigation, and of reflection. The same is true of learning to read judgments, whether for study within a wider framework or for a specific task in hand: to formulate grounds of appeal, or to derive support for an argument. But whatever that task is, the starting point is to read, to absorb facts and recognise argument, to reflect, consider, cogitate, ruminate, analyse and to reach the desired and necessary level of understanding to be able to apply your thoughts about the information provided.

In this context the *Adler*[1] method and classification of different levels of reading[2] is of particular assistance to the lawyer, since that is what we all engage in daily: whether substantive law, articles, textbooks, journals, documents or materials, we all read them inspectionally, analytically and syntopically whether or not we recognise such terms. We devote our time to the critical analysis of such material with a view to deciding whether it is relevant and whether we can apply it to assist us in solving the problem that presents itself.

This section then, is devoted to a discussion of the techniques involved in reading judgments, and to improve the skills of those who already practice such techniques.

FOCUS

Let us first recognise that judgments are intellectually taxing. They are not meant for light reading; they are of significance, and not just to the parties.

---

[1] *How to Read a Book* Adler & Van Doren (Touchstone 1972) pp 16–44.
[2] 'Elementary' 'inspectional' 'analytical' and 'syntopical'.

Some are entirely fact orientated and can readily be understood and applied at a single reading. However there are those of such weight and intellectual force as to be truly perplexing to anyone but a sophisticated reader of such matter.

Second, we should not lose sight of the fact that judgments have specific but different audiences. First the parties themselves; then, their legal teams. If coming from an appellate jurisdiction, first instance judges, or tribunal chairmen and members who will have to apply the decision or procedure ruled upon at subsequent hearings. If coming from the House of Lords or the European Court of Justice, a wider audience still – politicians, the media, the general public; and students of the law.

Third, the study of judgments already requires some degree of specialist skill in a number of different respects: they are not for the elementary reader, requiring a standard of English language and usage which is sufficient to carry understanding of sophisticated terms, phrases and words, including technical and professional jargon which is outside common parlance. They require some degree of understanding of basic legal principles, and more often than not, a degree of legal speciality.

Thus we should not characterise the reading of judgments as a commonplace, everyday or mundane activity. And that being so, it is important to see that as an activity it requires concentration, often intense concentration. The reader should therefore first find a time and a place where he can engage in difficult study without disturbance.

Some lawyers, whether out of habit or experience are able to read judgments on public transport, or with a musical accompaniment, or amid the hustle of a busy office, or whilst eating. They are lucky, or foolish, or both, and not an example to be followed. Find somewhere uninterrupted by distraction where you can give the material in question the concentration and effort it deserves.

TIME

A judgment should be read in its entirety in one sitting. Where the court consists of two or more judges, each of whom has delivered a separate judicial opinion because he has something of significance to say, preferably these should be read together at the same time. It is important that the reader has a feel for the whole of what is being said, since to approach it piecemeal, as well as breaking concentration, is more likely to encourage findings, argument and propositions of law being taken out of their true context, with the consequence of undermining a proper evaluation.

That is, of course, easier said than done. Important appeal judgments tend to be fairly lengthy. First-instance judgments which relate and then decide complex issues of fact, the subject of a trial lasting perhaps many days, may run to dozens if not a hundred pages or more. To read these in one sitting takes both planning and a deliberate effort to make the time available. Even a superficial reading of a judgment that one has not seen before may take a minute per page. For a close reading where one is trying to absorb facts, arguments, findings and law, you should allow up to three minutes per page, and with hard law, perhaps five minutes per page. Analytical reading often requires more than one examination.

The time that a lawyer takes in reading a judgment depends on what he is reading it for; upon his particular need; on what, if anything, he expects to find; and on what mechanical process he uses to record his findings. These factors will also determine the level of his reading, or to put it another way the depth of his conscious activity. Ordinarily the reader will have either a fixed or general purpose in addressing the judgment in question: he may be a general reader of all law reports or judgments that come his way, for example a subscriber to an issue of law reports that he takes the trouble to read before shelving; or he may be alerted, these days electronically, to every recent judgment in a designated broad sphere of interest. For reading at this level, known as *inspectional reading*, some judgments are hardly worth even skimming: the facts may be extreme and the decision wholly fact orientated; a quick glance may be sufficient to tell the reader this is not a relevant judgment or one worthy of mental retention for the task in hand.

INSPECTIONAL READING

Reading at the inspectional or general level does not require you to grasp every point on every page, nor should you wish to do so at this stage of your analysis: by mastering the finer points there is a risk that the big points may be missed. At this level only an outline of the wood is required, and seeing too many individual trees should not obscure this. If, however, the lawyer faces a very specific issue with which to deal, an argument that needs support, a problem that needs a solution, or a particular case that he has been referred to, then his level of alertness even at the inspectional reading stage will be different.

Inspectional reading is limited to answering the questions, what is this judgment about and is it relevant to answering my problem? But here he is likely to be making notes, perhaps both a citation reference and the briefest digest of the key facts. As he works syntopically, comparing the worth of what may be a number of judgments in the same area, towards eliminating the extraneous, the irrelevant and other unhelpful material, he anticipates the next level of reading, namely the *analytical*. This will be the most important exercise, enabling him to use the contents of the judgment as a building block to advance a legal proposition in support of his argument, or to detract from the argument of his opponent, or to deconstruct a judgment in which a finding has been made against his client, for the purpose of mounting an appeal, or to further a commercial endeavour in his client's interest. It is also the process which is most time-consuming and mentally absorbing.

3.2

THE MECHANICS OF ANALYTICAL READING

Analytical reading involves the close and careful study of the text with a questioning mind. Since at its most basic a judgment is merely the expression of a judicial opinion, the reader is not obliged to accept that opinion at face value. Subject to the doctrines of precedent, *stare decisis*, and *res judicata*[3] a judgment does not operate as holy writ, and the lawyer is free to agree or disagree with what he is reading. Even if his client's position appears to be subject to binding decided authority, he is still free intellectually to disagree with it.

Adler[4] suggests that reading beyond the elementary is essentially an effort on the part of the reader to ask of the reading matter questions, and to answer them to the best of the reader's ability. To identify what the material is about, first as a whole, and then what is being said in detail and how it is being said. Then whether it is true, and if so, whether in whole or in part; and if so, what is the effect of that truth – particularly what is the effect of that truth on the mind of the reader? He propounds the theory that understanding is a two-way operation in which reading should be a conversation between reader and author, where the learner has to question both himself and the teacher, and this includes arguing with propositions contained in the work.

The analytical reading of judgments requires an application of thought of some depth. The lawyer needs to familiarise himself with the text. He needs to establish what he accepts and what he rejects, and to apply this task equally to the court's findings of fact, the judge's arguments, whether his own or taken from counsel, and his propositions of law. He needs to ascertain and understand both the linguistic and logical basis for the judge's decision and to consider whether the judgment as a whole is consistent with basic principles and follows any recent trend in that area of the law, or whether it may fairly be

---

[3] The application of the rule *res judicata pro veritate accipitur* states that a judgment of a court of record must be taken as conclusive proof of the matter so decided: whether the rule is confined to the parties to the judgment or to all the world is the area for argument.

[4] *Op.cit* p.47.

criticised as inconsistent and out of step. This process may be made easier by applying a mechanistic approach such as set out afterwards.

Judgments should be read analytically in hard copy rather than electronically, either having been printed out or photocopied. This enables you, the reader, to mark them up, which of itself forms an important means of absorbing information and articulating where you agree or disagree. Major points or important or forceful statements should be underlined or highlighted. Vertical lines at the margin can be used to point up a passage which is too long to be underlined. References or cross-referenced annotation can be pointed up by using a star, asterisk or place number in the margin. Key words or phrases should be circled; questions can be written in the margin or at the top or foot of the page, with these being answered either by cross-referencing to another page, or perhaps overleaf. Expressions of agreement or disagreement should be stated, whether robustly or otherwise.

This process is of course, individual, and will no doubt be very familiar to students who have exercised such techniques throughout their academic studies. It is designed to release the thought patterns by which the analysis is being made and get them onto the page. In reading judgments analytically you should not be frightened to be aggressive with the text, since you are reaching beyond the assessment of facts to the evaluation of legal ideas and principles.

3.3
FORM AND STRUCTURE

Since 11th January 2001 it has been very much easier to analyse the structure and form of judgments emanating from the Supreme Court (a body which, unbeknown to the present Government, was created in 1875). Since that date all judgments in every division of the High Court and the Court of Appeal have been prepared for delivery, or issued as approved judgments, with single spacing, and paragraph numbering (in the margins) but no page numbers in compliance with the Lord Chief Justice's *Practice Statement*.[5] In courts with more than one judge, the paragraph numbering continues sequentially through each judgment, and does not start again at the beginning of the second judgment. Indented paragraphs are not given a number. This change was to facilitate the publication of judgments online, their subsequent use by the increasing numbers of those who have access to the Web, the creation of media-neutral citation references, and to assist those who use and wish to search judgments stored on electronic databases.

This movement towards consistency of form also extended to all judgments prepared for delivery, or issued as approved judgments in county courts. These were also directed to contain paragraph numbering (in the margins).

As a matter of usual practice then, judgments will be divided into numbered paragraphs and approved by the judge. There may also be headings and sectional divisions included for assistance. These are a useful guide to the content of parts of a judgment, since if there, they are included by the judge himself, although they should only be treated as one would the marginal notes in a statute.

Unlike Britain, the use of footnotes in judicial opinion has been the subject of a wide and long-lasting debate in the United States and the Commonwealth. These first appeared in the U.S. Supreme Court judgments of the late 1880s, although some 30 years later Justice Brandeis and Chief Justice Oliver Wendell

---

[5] Practice Direction (Judgments: Form and neutral citation) CA: Lord Woolf CJ: 11 January 2001; *The Times* 16 January 2001.

Holmes disapproved their use, and that of headings. In spite of that footnotes are now a recognised feature of judicial style in the United States, and, much more recently, in the High Court of Australia. In reporting the judicial opinions of South Africa's Constitutional Court observations which do not form part of the judgment are placed in the body of the opinion but in parenthesis. The higher courts of New Zealand and Canada have, thus far, resisted the use of footnotes.

There are other tools that have found favour in Commonwealth judgments now being used in written judgments handed down in England and Wales. These include tables of contents, for example at the commencement of the judgment of Hirst LJ in *Three Rivers District Council v Bank of England (No.3)*,[6] summaries or schedules of damages, such as in *Amstrad v Seagate*,[7] tables of currencies and exchange rates, as in *Lesotho Highlands DA v Impregilo SpA*,[8] and even engineering diagrams and collision charts: see *The "Kumanovo" and "Massira"*.[9] These feature most prominently in claims heard in the Technology & Construction Court, Admiralty Court and the Patent Court. In June, 2004 Lord Steyn issued an appendix to his speech in *Ghaidan v Godin-Mendoza (FC)*[10] listing all known cases in which the courts had reinterpreted statutes under the Human Rights Act and all cases where they had felt unable to do so. This appears to be the first time that an appendix has been provided with judicial opinion in the House of Lords.

---

[6] [2003] 2 AC 1 CA @ 18.
[7] (1997) 86 BLR 34 per HH Judge Lloyd QC @ 69.
[8] [2003] BLR 98 per Morison J @ 104.
[9] [1998] 2 Lloyd's Rep. 301 per Clarke J @ 316.
[10] [2004] UKHL 30.

3.4

PREPARING AN ANALYSIS

As a piece of writing a judgment should have unity, clarity and coherence and an orderly disposition of its contents. If that is so it should be possible to create a methodical analysis[11] which can be applied to any judgment irrespective of the complexity of the facts or the area of law under consideration. This can be reduced to a series of principles divided into stages of classification, interpretation and deconstruction.

CLASSIFICATION

1. Classify the judgment according to its weight of authority, purpose and subject matter:
    (a) note the level of jurisdiction;
    (b) note the constitution and seniority of the members of the bench;
    (c) establish whether the judgment is given *ex tempore* or is the subject of a reserved judgment. If the latter, note the delay between the close of the evidence and the handing down of the judgment;
    (d) consider whether the judgment is concerned with a procedural matter, a substantive interim application by which the outcome of the entire claim is being determined, or the determination of a full trial;
    (e) identify the area of law involved, first widely and then with progressively narrower focus;
    (f) consider whether the court as constituted had special knowledge of the area of law involved;
    (g) identify whether the judgment is fact orientated or the subject of wider judicial pronouncement;
    (h) identify whether the result is dependent on the exercise by the Court of a discretion.

---

[11] See *Adler's* Stages of Analytical Reading, *op.cit.* p.163–4.

2. Create a digest of what you think the whole judgment is about with the utmost brevity.

3. Dissect the major parts of the judgment by reference to their approved paragraph numbers and make a digest of these parts as you have outlined the whole.

4. Identify, using the judge's words or define using your own words, the problem or problems the judge is trying to solve.

INTERPRETATION

5. Locate the key sentences in the judgment which concern the problem or problems the judge is trying to solve; derive from such sentences the judge's key words.

6. Locate the judge's leading propositions by dealing with his most important sentences. These should concern:
   (a) reasons for his findings of fact;
   (b) the judge's view of the basic principles underlying the area of law with which he is dealing;
   (c) his view of the law applicable to these facts;
   (d) his application of the law to these facts;
   (e) the basis for the exercise, if any, of his discretion.

7. Understand the judge's arguments by finding them in, or constructing them out of, sequences of the important sentences or key words.

8. Identify which of his problems the judge has solved; and which, if any, he has not. Of the latter, decide whether the judge knows he has failed to solve a problem or problems and chosen so to do.

DECONSTRUCTION

9. Do not begin criticism until you have completed your classification and interpretation of the judgment. It is not possible to say that you agree, or disagree or even consciously to suspend judgment until you can say I understand the judge's arguments and his reasoning in making his findings and exercising any discretion.

10. Do not disagree contentiously. The basis of disagreement must be logic and not mere quarrel, since logic is necessary to mount the argument upon which any disagreement should be based.

11. Demonstrate that you can recognise the difference between knowledge and mere personal opinion by being in a position to present sound reasons for any critical judgment you make. This reasoning depends upon your ability to identify fair and proper criticism where it can properly be said that
    (a) the judge is uninformed;

(b) the judge is misinformed;

(c) the judge is illogical;

(d) the judge's analysis or account is incomplete.[12]

---

[12] These four propositions will be examined in greater detail below in Part 4: Analysing Judgments: Techniques for Criticism.

3.5
SYNTOPICAL READING

The process of syntopical reading involves the evaluation of two or more
pieces of writing on the same subject simultaneously. Lawyers probably
occupy their time engaged in syntopical reading more than any other group.
How often is your desk awash with different law reports, judgments and textbooks open at the same time, to enable the picking out of propositions and
dicta to support a position or create an argument. An electronic search may
also result in having a number of documents open on screen at the same time.

For practical purposes the lawyer uses syntopical reading as a journey,
progressing towards a narrow focal point. Accordingly, when researching a
problem you will know in broad terms the body of law which is the subject of
your search. You assume that more than one judgment is or may be relevant to
your need. You know that the task is to reduce your potentially long list of
authorities to the key cases, the key judgments, and the key passages which
will support your argument or undermine that of your opponent. If you are
searching electronically or start by using an indexing catalogue, your quest
will be language based, ever reducing your field using key phrases and key
words, until ending up with the relevant possibilities.

There are two problems which are fundamental: where to start and what to
read? These come about because legal practice is time sensitive. There is a real
risk that time taken in the syntopical reading of relevant books and relevant
passages to find the principal support for your propositions may exceed the
time available to undertake the analytical reading process. What is worse than
relying on a judgment that ever so slightly misses the key point, because
having found it during a syntopic process and assumed that it was on point,
insufficient time was available to analyse it?

The place to start therefore depends on the time available. An index or an electronic search, or the footnotes or substantive passages in an authoritative
textbook on the subject, will throw up a list of authorities, some of which may
be familiar and some unknown to you. A standard textbook may give some
idea of the breadth of subject matter available, and outline the basic principles.

The next exercise is to reduce the list to a manageable size. This is done by inspectional reading: a brief perusal of each authority will enable the skilful reader to discover whether the judgment has anything important to say about the problem in hand. It enables a number of cases to be discarded; it assists not only with the construction of your case, but you are very likely to discover the key authorities that your opponent will use.

Adler[13] considered that there should be definite steps in syntopical reading, although in applying his concept to your analysis of judgments, the order is necessarily different:

1. Have a clear idea of the problem which requires support;
    - try to abstract it to a simple sentence;
    - from that define the issues;
    - allow for any different conceptions of the question or potentially different views of the subject.
2. Understand that the process is concerned with discovery by reduction:
    - identify the area of law;
    - identify the key principles;
    - identify the available authorities;
    - arrange the cases in order by classification;
    - remove those that fall outside the classification.
3. Identify the relevant passages in the judgments.
4. Locate the key words or phrases and assess how the judge uses them. These must relate to the terms that you have searched, and are common to the cases under analysis. The use of such terms needs to be neutral between sources. Create a summary using the judge's own key words and phrases.
5. Accept the fact that sometimes the authority gives no answer to one or more of the problems or questions that you face.
6. Analyse the discussion to see what is relevant and assists, and what is relevant and does not assist. Discard that which you now consider to be irrelevant, understanding why that is. You may find assistance in the conflict between opposing answers where you have to consider and be able to explain how and why certain questions are answered by the judges differently.
7. Try and remain objective about conflicting opinions and arguments. At the stage of syntopical reading you are concentrating on the relevance and worth of a judgment, not whether you accept what is being said. Concentrate on the actual words used by the judges to ensure that any citation is strictly accurate.

---

[13] *Op.cit.* p. 316.

PART 4
THE USE OF LANGUAGE IN JUDGMENTS

4
THE USE OF LANGUAGE IN JUDGMENTS

Lawyers dealing with contentious business exercise three basic skills – critical analysis, problem solving and communication. Judges extend critical analysis into making value judgments, and develop problem solving into decision-making. However the skill of communication remains the same: it is the essence of delivering the judgment. It is, of course, language based, English being a particularly rich and expressive language in which to couch small differences of nuance in tone, colour and mood. The care with which words are chosen to formulate judgments is of immense importance to the judiciary, and the more senior the tribunal the greater the care with which each clause and each sentence is taken becomes greater. Each word has its place, whether used in the kind of memorable lyrical opening for which Lord Denning was famous, such as in *Hinz* v *Berry* [1970] 2 QB 40 @ 42:

> "It happened on April 19, 1964. It was bluebell time in Kent. Mr. and Mrs. Hinz had been married some 10 years, and they had four children, all aged nine and under. The youngest was one. Mrs. Hinz was a remarkable woman. In addition to her own four, she was foster-mother to four other children. To add to it, she was two months pregnant with her fifth child.
>
> On this day they drove out in a Bedford Dormobile van from Tonbridge to Canvey Island. They took all eight children with them. As they were coming back they turned into a lay-by at Thurnham to have a picnic tea. The husband, Mr. Hinz, was at the back of the Dormobile making the tea. Mrs. Hinz had taken Stephanie, her third child, aged three, across the road to pick bluebells on the opposite side. There came along a Jaguar car driven by Mr. Berry, out of control. A tyre had burst. The Jaguar rushed into this lay-by and crashed into Mr. Hinz and the children. Mr. Hinz was frightfully injured and died a little later. Nearly all the children were hurt. Blood was streaming from their heads. Mrs. Hinz, hearing the crash, turned round and saw

this disaster. She ran across the road and did all she could. Her husband was beyond recall. But the children recovered.

An action has been brought on her behalf and on behalf of the children for damages against Mr. Berry, the defendant. The injuries to the children have been settled by various sums being paid. The pecuniary loss to Mrs. Hinz by reason of the loss of her husband has been found by the judge to be some £15,000; but there remains the question of the damages payable to her for her nervous shock – the shock which she suffered by seeing her husband lying in the road dying, and the children strewn about.'

or in *Lloyds Bank Plc* v *Bundy*[1]

'Broadchalke is one of the most pleasing villages in England. Old Herbert Bundy, the defendant, was a farmer there. His home was at Yew Tree Farm. It went back for 300 years. His family had been there for generations. It was his only asset. But he did a very foolish thing. He mortgaged it to the bank. Up to the very hilt. Not to borrow money for himself, but for the sake of his son. Now the bank have come down on him. They have foreclosed. They want to get him out of Yew Tree Farm and to sell it. They have brought this action against him for possession. Going out means ruin for him. He was granted legal aid. His lawyers put in a defence. They said that, when he executed the charge to the bank he did not know what he was doing: or at any rate that the circumstances were such that he ought not to be bound by it. At the trial his plight was plain. The judge was sorry for him. He said he was a "poor old gentleman." He was so obviously incapacitated that the judge admitted his proof in evidence. He had a heart attack in the witness-box. Yet the judge felt he could do nothing for him. There is nothing, he said, "which takes this out of the vast range of commercial transactions." He ordered Herbert Bundy to give up possession of Yew Tree Farm to the bank. Now there is an appeal to this court. The ground is that the circumstances were so exceptional that Herbert Bundy should not be held bound.'

or a pithy aphorism, such as

'the state of a man's mind is as much a fact as the state of his digestion'[2]

or a pragmatic rhetorical statement in the form of question and self-answer:

---

[1] [1975] QB 326 @ 334
[2] *Edgington* v *Fitzmauraice* (1889) 29 Ch.D. 459 per Bowen LJ @ 483

'Does section 36(1) of the 1993 Act prohibit the making of a contract for the sale of charity land?

27 But for the decision in *Milner v Staffordshire Congregational Union (Inc)* [1956] Ch 275 I would have no doubt that the answer to the question whether section 36(1) of the 1993 Act prohibits the making (as distinct from the performance) of a contract for the sale of charity land–in circumstances where section 36(1) applies–is "No".'[3]

In his insightful article *A Matter of Style*[4] Professor Markesinis argued, when contrasting English, American and German judicial styles, that the use of language gave the common law judgment its special features and distinctive edge, and that style, in the judicial context, can tell the careful observer a great deal about the judicial process, the judge, and the real issues confronting him in a legal dispute. But, he says, "how a person speaks depends upon whom he is addressing; and we know not in England – let alone in other systems – to whom the judges are addressing their remarks."[5]

When asked what they considered their function to be in delivering a judgment, the judges with whom I have spoken identified a range of audiences. First instance judges and tribunal chairmen point to the need to provide the parties and their lawyers with a final decision of the matter in hand and to explain clearly their reasons for it, particularly ensuring that the loser understands why he has lost. Where a litigant is in person the reasoning, jargon and legal concepts must be explained in a way that a layman can readily understand. For lawyers the reasoning must be coherent and logical; it must convey a sense of impartial and comprehensive analysis of the evidence and argument of all sides.

Lords Justices of Appeal considered it important, in addition, to make their decision clear to lawyers and other judges who would have to read it and apply what was, and equally what was not, decided. Or as Sir Christopher Staughton puts it:[6]

'there is a good deal to be said for certainty in the law, for at least two reasons. First, people ought to know, or be able to find out, whether their future conduct will be lawful or not...Secondly, uncertainty in the law breeds litigation."

---

[3] *Bayoumi v Women's Total Abstinence Union Ltd* [2003] EWCA Civ 1548 [2004] Ch 46 per Chadwick LJ @57
[4] (1994) 110 LQR 607.
[5] ibid p.608.
[6] *What's Wrong with the Law in the Year 2000* Inner Temple Millennium Lecture given by the Rt. Hon Sir Christopher Staughton.

The audience intended for a dissenting judgment is invariably, as well as the parties and their lawyers, a higher court or perhaps a specialist branch of the profession.

Lords of Appeal in Ordinary and members of the Judicial Committee of the Privy Council strive to create judicial opinion that is practical in application, intellectually satisfying and stimulating of policy debate.

Recognising then, that the judiciary is addressing different audiences, let us consider the practical means by which linguistic analysis can be of assistance in breaking down a judgment. This is an exercise that goes back to the earliest of lessons in grammar and syntax.

4.1
LINGUISTIC ANALYSIS

Sound legal argument should be based on a series of propositions, each supported by the requisite authority or the necessary evidence, in a progression that creates a momentum driving the recipient inexorably to the desired conclusion. The progression should flow both linguistically and logically. Where the support is either illusory or insufficient, or where the progression is illogical, the argument will break down as the momentum towards the desired conclusion falters. If the argument is contained in a judgment, it is at this point that the judgment becomes open to fair criticism, and hence an appeal.

Look first at the linguistic progression of argument contained in a judgment: lawyers have to examine sentences with care, much in the same way as analysing pleadings, to see what can be accepted and what must be denied. *Adler* suggests[7] an essential part of reading is to be perplexed and to wonder. If you do not question the meaning of a passage how can you gain the insight you do not already possess?

To do so you have to become aware of the key words and phrases, which begs the question how do you locate the most important sentences in a judgment, and analyse the propositions they contain? In considering non-fiction generally *Adler* deals[8] with the problem thus:

> "...The important sentences are the ones that express the judgments on which (the author's) whole argument rests. A book usually contains much more than the bare statement of an argument, or a series of arguments. The author may explain how he came to the point of view he now holds ... he may comment on the work of others ... he may indulge in all sorts of supporting and surrounding discussion. But the heart of his communication lies in the major affirmations and denials he is making and the reasons he gives for doing

---

7 *Op. cit.* p.123.
8 *Op. cit.* p. 121.

so. To come to grips, therefore, you have to see the main sentences as if they were raised from the page in high relief. Some authors help you do this. They underline the sentences for you ... tell you that this is an important point when they make it, or they use another typographical device to make their leading sentences stand out ... there are a few books in which the leading propositions are set forth in sentences that occupy a special place in the order and style of the exposition."

There are now many stylistic ways in which judges point up the principal thrust of their arguments to assist the reader. Some are copied or developed typographically by law reporters. These include the use of the now common sectional headings or labels which appear in lengthy judgments. Or as we have seen, there might be the rhetorical question in which the judge poses the question which he then goes on to answer, for example:

"The question the county court judge should have asked himself was this: Would an ordinary man, addressing his mind to the question whether [the daughter] was a member of the family or not, have answered 'Yes' or 'No'? To that question I think there is only one possible answer, and that is 'Yes.'"[9]

Alternatively the judge may call attention to a conclusion, having weighed up the conflicting authorities or the competing evidence: see Lord Phillips of Worth Matravers MR in *In re S* [2003] EWCA Civ 963 [2004] Fam 43 @ [111] citing the trial judge Hedley J below:

"18. In the end, and not without a degree of regret, I have concluded that this proviso must remain in the injunction and that I should not prevent the reporting of the name of the defendant and the identity of the deceased child as her son. My regret is engendered by the recognition that these will be dreadfully painful times for CS.

19. The essence of my reasons for that conclusion are as follows. First I recognise the primacy in a democratic society of the open reporting of public proceedings on grave criminal charges and the inevitable price that that involves in incursions on the privacy of individuals. Secondly, I recognise that Parliament has in a number of statutes qualified that right to report and, in the context of this case, most notably in section 39 of the 1933 Act; where a set of circumstances arise not covered by those provisions the court should in my judgment be slow to extend the incursion into the right of free speech by the use of the

---

[9] *Brock* v *Wollams* [1949] 2 K.B. 388 per Cohen L.J. at p. 395.

inherent jurisdiction. Thirdly, I have to recognise that not even the restrictions contended for here offer real hope to CS of proper isolation from the fallout of publicity at this trial; it is inevitable that those who know him will identify him and thus frustrate the purpose of the restriction. Last, I am simply not convinced that, when everything is drawn together and weighed, it can be said that grounds under article 10(2) of the Convention have been made out in terms of the balance of the effective preservation of CS's article 8 rights against the right to publish under article 10. I should add, although it is not strictly necessary to do so, that I think I would have come to the same conclusion even had I been persuaded that this was a case where CS's welfare was indeed my paramount consideration under section 1(1) of the 1989 Act."

Sometimes, helpfully, he will set out numbered principles, perhaps drawn from existing case law and then add his own or apply the reasoning to suit the facts before him. Good examples are the speech of Lord Hoffman in *Investors Compensation Scheme Ltd* v *West Bromwich Building Society*:[10]

"I think I should preface my explanation of my reasons with some general remarks about the principles by which contractual documents are nowadays construed. I do not think that the fundamental change which has overtaken this branch of the law, particularly as a result of the speeches of Lord Wilberforce in *Prenn* v *Simmonds* [1971] 1 W.L.R. 1381, 1384–1386 and *Reardon Smith Line Ltd.* v *Yngvar Hansen-Tangen* [1976] 1 W.L.R. 989, is always sufficiently appreciated. The result has been, subject to one important exception, to assimilate the way in which such documents are interpreted by judges to the common sense principles by which any serious utterance would be interpreted in ordinary life. Almost all the old intellectual baggage of "legal" interpretation has been discarded. The principles may be summarised as follows.

(1) Interpretation is the ascertainment of the meaning which the document would convey to a reasonable person having all the background knowledge which would reasonably have been available to the parties in the situation in which they were at the time of the contract.

(2) The background was famously referred to by Lord Wilberforce as the "matrix of fact," but this phrase is, if anything, an understated description of what the background may include. Subject to the

---

[10] [1998] 1 WLR 896 @ 912H.

requirement that it should have been reasonably available to the parties and to the exception to be mentioned next, it includes absolutely anything which would have affected the way in which the language of the document would have been understood by a reasonable man.

(3) The law excludes from the admissible background the previous negotiations of the parties and their declarations of subjective intent. They are admissible only in an action for rectification. The law makes this distinction for reasons of practical policy and, in this respect only, legal interpretation differs from the way we would interpret utterances in ordinary life. The boundaries of this exception are in some respects unclear. But this is not the occasion on which to explore them.

(4) The meaning which a document (or any other utterance) would convey to a reasonable man is not the same thing as the meaning of its words. The meaning of words is a matter of dictionaries and grammars; the meaning of the document is what the parties using those words against the relevant background would reasonably have been understood to mean. The background may not merely enable the reasonable man to choose between the possible meanings of words which are ambiguous but even (as occasionally happens in ordinary life) to conclude that the parties must, for whatever reason, have used the wrong words or syntax: see *Mannai Investments Co. Ltd.* v *Eagle Star Life Assurance Co. Ltd.* [1997] A.C. 749.

(5) The "rule" that words should be given their "natural and ordinary meaning" reflects the common sense proposition that we do not easily accept that people have made linguistic mistakes, particularly in formal documents. On the other hand, if one would nevertheless conclude from the background that something must have gone wrong with the language, the law does not require judges to attribute to the parties an intention which they plainly could not have had. Lord Diplock made this point more vigorously when he said in *Antaios Compania Naviera S.A.* v *Salen Rederierna A.B.* [1985] A.C. 191, 201:

> "if detailed semantic and syntactical analysis of words in a commercial contract is going to lead to a conclusion that flouts business commonsense, it must be made to yield to business commonsense."

If one applies these principles, it seems to me that the judge must be right and, as we are dealing with one badly drafted clause which is happily no longer in use, there is little advantage in my repeating his reasons at greater length."

and per Mummery J. in *Tyldesley* v *TML Plastics*[11]

"In our view, the legal position is as follows.

(1) The Equal Pay Act 1970, article 119 of the E.C. Treaty (O.J. 1992 No. C.224) and the Equal Pay Directive (Council Directive (75/117/E.E.C.)) have as their purpose the elimination of sex discrimination, not that of achieving "fair wages." Their detailed provisions are to be construed in the light of that purpose.

(2) A difference in pay explained by a factor not itself a factor of sex, or tainted by sex discrimination, should, in principle, constitute a valid defence.

(3) The comment of the House of Lords in *Rainey* v *Greater Glasgow Health Board* [1987] I.C.R. 129, 145, that, in order to establish the defence under section 1(3) of the Act of 1970, objective justification must be shown, applies only where, as on the facts of *Rainey*, the factor to be relied upon is one which affects a considerably higher proportion of women than men, so as to be indirectly discriminatory and thus tainted by sex discrimination, unless justified. The same observation may be made in relation to the comments of the Court of Justice in *Jenkins* v *Kingsgate (Clothing Productions) Ltd. (Case 96/80)* [1981] I.C.R. 592 and *Enderby* v *Frenchay Health Authority (Case C-127/92)* [1994] I.C.R. 112. Those were both cases where the factor relied upon was one which affected a considerably higher proportion of women than men and therefore required objective justification.

(4) Even if *Enderby* was not a case of indirect discrimination, as understood by English law, the pre-condition of enjoying a higher salary in that case was membership of a group which comprised predominantly men. A prima facie case of unequal treatment was made out which needed to be rebutted by objective justification. No such case arises here. There was no suggestion that the requirement of particular experience of, or embracing, total quality management was one which affected a considerably higher proportion of women than men.

(5) Accordingly, there was no allegation or evidence in this case of indirect discrimination which required rebuttal by objective justification.

---

[11] [1996] ICR 356 EAT @ 361.

(6) In the absence of evidence or a suggestion that the factor relied on to explain the differential was itself tainted by gender, because indirectly discriminatory or because it adversely impacted on women as a group in the sense indicated in *Enderby*, no requirement of objective justification arises: see *Calder* v *Rowntree Mackintosh Confectionery Ltd.* [1992] I.C.R. 372, 379–380F, and [1993] I.C.R. 811 and *Yorkshire Blood Transfusion Service* v *Plaskitt* [1994] I.C.R. 74, 79–80F. Thus, even if a differential is explained by careless mistake, which could not possibly be objectively justified, that would amount to a defence under section 1(3) and for the purpose of article 119 of the E.C. Treaty, provided that the tribunal is satisfied that the mistake was either the sole reason for it or of sufficient influence to be significant or relevant. If a genuine mistake suffices, so must a genuine perception, whether reasonable or not, about the need to engage an individual with particular experience, commitment and skills.

For those reasons, the industrial tribunal erred in law in directing itself that the explanation for the difference in pay had to be objectively justified. It was sufficient in law that the explanation itself caused the difference or was a sufficient influence to be significant and relevant, whether or not that explanation was objectively justified."

4.2

THE USE OF WORDS

Knowledge is communicated by the skilled use of words. Plainly in a judgment, even one considered and crafted by someone with as much skill as a Law Lord, some words are more important than others and these need to be located and their meaning determined with precision. They are the vehicles for argument and persuasion. These are the words that make a real difference in understanding the passage in which they occur, although their importance is not absolute but relative – it is a question of degree. For example such words may be used in common speech daily by the man in the street; he is familiar with their ambiguity and he has grown accustomed to the variation of their meanings as they occur in this context or that. However, irrespective of any technical legal meaning, even words in common parlance may be used in a definitely special sense. This is particularly true of statutory interpretation, which provides the judiciary with knotty problems arising out of the commonest of words, such as "can" which Lord Fraser of Tulleybelton had to examine in *Mandla v Dowell Lee* [1983] 2 AC 548 HL @ 565F when considering the funding of schools for Sikh children:

"Can comply"

It is obvious that Sikhs, like anyone else, "can" refrain from wearing a turban, if "can" is construed literally. But if the broad cultural/historic meaning of ethnic is the appropriate meaning of the word in the Act of 1976, then a literal reading of the word "can" would deprive Sikhs and members of other groups defined by reference to their ethnic origins of much of the protection which Parliament evidently intended the Act to afford to them. They "can" comply with almost any requirement or condition if they are willing to give up their distinctive customs and cultural rules. On the other hand, if ethnic means inherited or unalterable, as the Court of Appeal thought it did, then "can" ought logically to be read literally. The word "can" is used with many shades of meaning. In the context of section 1 (1) (*b*) (i) of the Act of 1976 it must, in my opinion, have been intended by Parliament to be read not as meaning "can physically," so as to indicate a theoretical possibility, but as meaning "can in practice" or "can consistently with the customs and cultural conditions of the racial group." The latter meaning was attributed to the word by the Employment Appeal Tribunal in *Price v Civil Service Commission* [1978] I.C.R. 27, on a construction of the parallel provision in the Sex Discrimination Act 1975. I agree with their construction of the word in that context. Accordingly I am of opinion that the "No turban" rule was not one with which the second appellant could, in the relevant sense, comply.

How the word in question is to be understood makes a difference that both the lawyer as reader and the judge as writer must be concerned with. The failure of clarity in communication leading to the absence of a party understanding with precision the meaning of words used is often the cause of difficulty in interpretation, in ascertaining relevance, and in formulating issues, for example for an appeal. Often in appeals, where the facts are fixed, the losing party has asked the court to determine (or indeed the judge below had fixed) what is in effect, and perhaps only slightly, the wrong question.

By way of example this occurred in *Daniels v Thompson*,[12] a case alleging solicitor's negligence in providing estate tax planning advice resulting in liability for the payment of inheritance tax which the testator client had sought to avoid. Here the district judge had ordered the trial of these preliminary issues on limitation:

"on what date did the claimant's cause of action accrue and on what date will/does the primary limitation period expire? If the primary limitation period has expired, when was the claimant's knowledge and on what date will/does the limitation period pursuant to section 14A of the Limitation Act 1980 expire?"

In the Court of Appeal the judges rapidly identified the preliminary issues as avoiding the correct question for the court to decide, namely whether the claimant had a cause of action as pleaded at all. Lord Justice Dyson explains:

"[32.] It is important to keep in mind that the preliminary issue before the court was limited to the question when Mrs Daniels first suffered loss, and did not embrace the separate question whether the liability for inheritance tax on the transfer of Thornfield was a loss that was suffered by Mrs Daniels. I confess, however, that I have found it impossible to resist the temptation to consider at least whether Mrs Daniels could have suffered the alleged loss. In my view, it is artificial in a case such as this to consider when a person first suffers loss

---

[12] [2004] EWCA Civ 307;[2004] PNLR 33.

without deciding whether she was at least capable of suffering that loss.

[33.] I shall explain why in my judgment Mrs Daniels could not have suffered the alleged loss as a result of the defendant's alleged negligence."

How then do you find the important or key words in a judgment? Since your object is to read for understanding you must be concerned with the ideas of the judge. The grammatical structure of what is being expressed may therefore become important. In construing the intention of the judge in delivering his judgment, basic rules of grammar must be regarded: you should have regard to the role of adjectives and adverbs, how verbs function in relation to nouns, how modifying words and clauses restrict or amplify the meaning of the words they qualify; you must be able to dissect a sentence according to the rules of syntax.[13]

This will include:

●   Identifying the key propositions that are being advanced by the judge, or drawn from counsel's submissions and are being accepted as correct.

●   Separating out all of the different, though related, propositions and trying to put them in your own words to see that you have the meaning right.

●   Locating and underlining or highlighting the principal words or clauses that drive forward the proposition.

●   Establishing whether these words are used elsewhere in passages in the judgment or are drawn from either authority relied upon in support of the proposition or the evidence.

●   Noting from the context whether the words have any specialist or technical meaning, or if words in common speech, any particularly narrow focus.

●   If you do not understand a particular word search out its meaning in the wider context of the whole judgment, although you should accept that if the context is built around the word used in a particular way that may be of no assistance, and you will need to have recourse to a specialist dictionary.

In looking at the use of words let us start by postulating, reasonably, that a judge uses most words as men ordinarily do in conversation with a range of meanings and trusting to the context to indicate any divergence from their

---

[13] See *Adler* op. cit. at p. 125.

established sense. This is particularly so in judgments delivered *ex tempore* without prior construction or to litigants in person. In these situations the judge's style is likely to be formal but conversational; in the latter he will try to be non-legalistic. A transcript of such a judgment should cause no analytical problems. The difficulty arises where judges use words which create an ambiguity due to complicated or extended sentence structure, jargon-ridden terminology, contemporary, technical and specialist vocabulary, arcane literary style or techniques more designed for literary effect. The passage that resounds and is marvellous to read, but you are not entirely sure what the judge means by it, or whether the assumed meaning is quite right.

Members of the judiciary are not shy of using long and complex sentences: here is Mr Justice Sachs on indictments:

"The first point that becomes quite clear upon an examination of the authorities is that questions of joinder, be they of offences or of offenders, are matters of practice on which the court has, unless restrained by statute, inherent power both to formulate its own rules and to vary them in the light of current experience and the needs of justice. Thus in *Reg.* v *Tizard* it was specifically stated that the relative principles have been evolved as rules of practice, and attention was drawn to the fact that the court need not be astute so to define the rules as to preclude joinders in view of the overall discretion of the judge to order separate trials where the interests of justice so required...This court has said more than once that counts simply charging the several accused individually with particular offences committed are often to be preferred to counts, such as conspiracy, which involve the establishment of some additional element of acting in concert; that, however, was largely with a view to simplifying the issues to be placed before the jury and that practice rule does not of itself provide any warrant for an accused saying that in the absence of such a count it is wrong that he should be tried with the other persons involved in the same series of incidents...Again, while the court has in mind the classes of case that have been particularly the subject of discussion before it, such as incidents which, irrespective of there appearing a joint charge in the indictment, are contemporaneous (as where there has been something in the nature of an affray), or successive (as in protection racket cases), or linked in a similar manner, as where two persons individually in the course of the same trial commit perjury as regards the same or a closely connected fact, the court does not intend the operation of the rule to be restricted so as to apply only to such cases as have been discussed before it."[14]

---

[14] *Reg.* v *Assim* [1966] 2 QB 249 @ 258 and 261.

and Lord Diplock on dredging rights in the River Thames:

> "The concept that there is such a thing as a "natural flow" of water that determines the configuration of the bed of a river with the consequence that it is, in law, a public nuisance to do anything that interferes with that configuration in such a way as to prevent vessels of a particular draught passing over a particular part of the surface of the water can have no application to a navigable river like the Thames, whose bed, soil and shore are vested in a statutory authority whose functions include the control of all navigation on the river and which is empowered itself to do, and to authorise riparian owners to do, acts on the bed of the river which inevitably affect the migration of silt from one part of the bed to another and cause changes in the previous configuration of the bed... Cessation of dredging at a particular place and removal of structures will inevitably affect the configuration of the bed of the river; and since such cessation or removal may lawfully be called for by the P.L.A. upon short notice at any time, a member of the public wishing to exercise his public right of navigation over a particular part of the water of the Thames has no public right to continue to find at that place a depth of water greater than it would have been if no dredging of the river had taken place there or a licensed structure had not been removed...(8) Before any construction work had started on the ferry terminals the depth of water at that part of the river where the jetty head of the raw sugar jetty was subsequently located was insufficient to permit of navigation by vessels of the draught that the raw sugar jetty was intended to accommodate; so at that time there could be no public right to navigate there in vessels of that draught. Dredging the bed of the river in that area to a depth sufficient to enable vessels of that draught to have access from the main navigational channel to the raw sugar jetty head and to moor there for the purpose of unloading raw sugar, whether such dredging was undertaken by the P.L.A. itself or by someone else licensed to undertake it by the P.L.A., could not, for the reasons stated in (7), give rise to any public right to the maintenance of that additional depth; and for the purpose of any cause of action for particular damage sustained in consequence of a public nuisance, which is the only cause of action to which your Lordships have held that Tate & Lyle are entitled, they must as a condition precedent to that cause of action establish that there has been an interference with a right of navigation to which *every* member of the public is entitled."[15]

---

[15] *Tate & Lyle v GLC* [1983] 2 AC 509 @ 546,547

4.3

THE STRUCTURE OF SENTENCES

When you come to analyse what you consider the most important sentences in a judgment these should be divided into classes:

- Declarative – sentences that express propositions, declarations of knowledge or opinion;

- Interrogative – sentences that ask questions;

- Sentences conveying wishes or intentions.

Not all declarative sentences can be read as if each expressed only one proposition. When its words are used unambiguously a simple sentence usually expresses a single proposition, but even grammatically simple sentences may contain two or more propositions, each of which must be considered. By no means are all simple sentences. Even when its words are used unambiguously a compound sentence can express two or more propositions, particularly those related in the form of an argument. You must break up the sentence, clause by clause, and see how the proposition is constructed. Decide whether there is any flaw in its logical progression. Grammatical single sentences may in fact be extremely complex as a result of the use of semicolons. Unless the separate and distinct propositions in a complicated sentence are recognised you cannot make a discriminating judgment on what is being said since it is perfectly possible to agree with one proposition but not with the others.[16]

Arguments tend to have a fluidity and movement. An argument begins somewhere, goes somewhere, and gets somewhere.[17] This is a movement of thought. It may begin with what is really the conclusion and then proceed to give reasons for it. Or it may start with the evidence and the reasons and bring you to the conclusion that should follow from it. Generally speaking a sentence within an argument must be either a premise or a conclusion. Usually a string of linked premises arrive at a conclusion by progression. Thus to find the key propositions you will ask the questions:

---

[16] See *Adler* op. cit. at p. 129.
[17] *Ibid* at p. 123.

- Is this a premise?

- Is it supported adequately by the evidence?

- Is a conclusion asserted?

- Does the conclusion flow satisfactorily from supported premises?

- Does this conclusion decide an identified issue?

- Does this conclusion belong to the main argument?

4.4

THE LANGUAGE OF LAWYERS

The law has a language of its own, and contains a vocabulary with an unusually large number of foreign phrases, derived principally from Norman French and medieval Latin, archaic words and expressions, and terms of art. It is at the same time formal, dignified and solemn while being expressive and evocative, and even quirky. It includes professional jargon, idiomatic expressions, and grammatical idiosyncrasies.

Language when used as a tool of work by practitioners is highly conventional: we lawyers recognise legal concepts within ordinary language because of our background, education and training, and hopefully, the precision with which we use words. This is particularly true of words that have several distinct meanings that can be used in either a single sense or a combination of senses for example "title", "consideration", "release" or "security". Since all judges are drawn from the ranks of experienced, qualified lawyers, even if not practising as advocates at the time of their elevation, there is no reason to suppose their use of language when dealing with fellow lawyers as an audience will be any different.

Within the confines of our profession we make extensive use of legal vocabulary or ordinary language used in a specialised way for several distinct purposes: as a convenient form of shorthand; to shield the contents of our discussion from laymen; to soften the impact of the adversarial nature of much of our work; and to speak with a degree of equality both to those more senior than us and with the judges. Although the Woolf reforms were intended to de-mystify legal jargon and make the use of the courts more consumer friendly, these purposes remain; and a distinct professional language is as necessary to lawyers as it is to the medical profession, or indeed the non-learned professions. It may be, as Lord Irvine LC suggested in presenting the Woolf reforms to the House of Lords that 'Lawyers therefore will have to talk to one another in Latin in private from now on,'[18] but at least in making that quip he recognised the need for lawyers to talk privately to

---

[18] Hansard 26 Apr 1999 : Column 6.

each other in a professional language. If the judge's audience continues to include his junior brethren and the lawyers who must appear before them, professional language will spill over into his judgment, and in my view rightly so. If it is the case that the judges are obliged to disapprove the use of a private professional language which is entirely appropriate in certain circumstances, they will strive to find an alternative which does not give rise to ambiguity, lack of precision or at least a debate over its construction. This is where, with great respect to Sir Ernest Gowers,[19] Bryan A. Garner[20] and Lord Woolf LCJ himself, the use of plain English in legal writing falls down, since simple language is often the most ambiguous. In formulating her views on whether the disclosure of matters raised in Family Division chambers hearings was contemptuous, Dame Butler-Sloss P, had to tackle the meaning of the words "private","chambers" and "in camera", and was driven to cite Humpty Dumpty:[21]

"**17** Proceedings in the courts are either held in open court, where the public is entitled to enter and listen or in circumstances in which the public is largely excluded either by rule of court or by practice. This exclusion does not, of itself, have the consequence of a ban on later publication. There was some confusion in argument in this court, as there has been in the past, as to the meaning given to the words "chambers", "private", or "in camera". I start with the meaning of the word "chambers". It is not defined in the Supreme Court Act 1981 which states, in section 67:

"Business in the High Court shall be heard and disposed of in court except in so far as it may, under this or any other Act, under rules of court or in accordance with the practice of the court, be dealt with in chambers."

18 In *The Supreme Court Practice 1997*, vol 2, p 1771, para 5276, "chambers" was contrasted with "in court" to mean "in private, secret, secluded behind closed doors". That definition was not considered an accurate description by Lord Woolf MR in *Hodgson* v *Imperial Tobacco Ltd* [1998] 1 WLR 1056, 1069. Jacob J in *Forbes* v *Smith* [1998] 1 All ER 973, 974 in the passage I cite below, treated "in chambers" as the same as "in private", as I did in *In re P-B (A Minor)(Child Cases: Hearings in Open Court)* [1997] 1 All ER 58, 59–62. Jacob J's definition was approved by Lord Woolf MR in *Hodgson's* case, at p 1069, and now adopted in CPR r 39.2: see paragraph 25 below.

[19] See *The Complete Plain Words* Gowers (Penguin 1990).
[20] See *Legal Writing in Plain English* Garner (Chicago 2001).
[21] *Clibbery* v *Allen* [2002] Fam 261 CA @ 270 [17]-[19].

19 The other phrase in use, in particular, in the Chancery Division, was "in camera". This phrase sometimes denoted proceedings which were confidential or secret with the effect that the public were excluded and in respect of which there could be no subsequent publication of information. That situation was recognised by Lord Woolf MR in *Hodgson's* case. The phrase sometimes meant the same as "in chambers". The exclusion of the public from the hearing, as such, did not necessarily have the effect of prohibiting later publication of the proceedings. In section 12(3) of the Administration of Justice Act 1960 hearings "in chambers" and "in camera" were treated equally: "references to a court sitting in private include references to a court sitting in camera or in chambers." That would appear also to be the case in adoption. In section 64 of the Adoption Act 1976 proceedings are held in private: "proceedings under this Act–(a) in the High Court, may be disposed of in chambers; (b) in a county court, shall be heard and determined in camera ..." I am driven to recall Humpty Dumpty: "When I use a word ... it means just what I choose it to mean–neither more nor less."

Nor is there any escaping the fact that many words in ordinary use have a highly technical meaning in law which may itself change depending on the context: "dishonest", "goodwill", "mistake" and "consideration", to suggest but a few. There is a limit to the guidance which general language can provide and consciously or unconsciously the use of general language excludes participation in the legal process.[22]

---

[22] See *The Role of Linguistics in Legal Analysis* Peter Goodrich (1984) 47 MLR 523.

4.5

CONTEMPORARY VOCABULARY AND SOCIAL CHANGE

The language we use is also anchored in time, and there is great danger in using slang, colloquialism or vulgarism in the course either of argument or in a judgment, even if drawn from the precise words used in evidence. Judicial style is often shaped by social and historical factors which may have lost some of their original force. Expressions that may have been common even twenty years ago may now seem obsolete, and words and phrases that were familiar items in daily usage when the judge was a young practitioner may cause a contemporary audience difficulty in detecting the meaning which he intended the use of the words to have. If that is true of phrases used within professional living memory, a judgment that is 100 or 150 years old will need to be analysed linguistically as a historical text.

Take for example the expression "living in sin", a fairly commonplace pejorative expression in use widely only twenty years ago. In 1998 judges were faced with the task of dealing with property rights of unmarried co-habitees as a consequence of drastic social change, and considered the applicable judicial terminology:[23]

> "Unmarried cohabitation between heterosexuals developed strikingly in scale to the point that today (according to figures helpfully supplied by the Family Policies Study Centre) 25 per cent. of all women aged between 18 and 49 are unmarried cohabitants, and in the age group most likely to cohabit (women in their late twenties and men in their late thirties) over one-third of the population now cohabits. As it became more common, cohabitation lost the secretiveness with which it had sometimes been concealed by those who felt the need to give the appearances of marriage (through change of surname by deed poll for example) to their relationship. As it became more open, so attitudes toward it became less judgmental. That

---

[23] *Fitzpatrick v Sterling Housing Association Ltd.* (C.A.) [1998] Ch. 304 per Waite L.J. @ 308.

included the attitude of the courts, where, notwithstanding that the encouragement of marriage as an institution remains a well established head of public policy, the respect due to the sincerity of commitment involved in many such relationships is reflected in judicial terminology – terms like "partner" now being more generally used than the once preferred references to "common law spouse," "mistress" or even (as will shortly be illustrated) "living in sin."[23]

It is true that every so often a judge will intentionally use archaic words or archaic senses of words, perhaps for the purpose of gravitas, or deliberately to resist a modern idiom which he may dislike, or occasionally to turn a mischievous nose up at the media and revel in being thought old-fashioned and aloof. However it is as well we remember that the law develops both substantively and linguistically with social change, and does not act as a buffer against it. The judges are the first to recognise this:

"No one really doubts that the common law is a body of law which develops in process of time in response to the developments of the society in which it rules. Its movement may not be perceptible at any distinct point of time, nor can we always say how it gets from one point to another; but I do not think that, for all that, we need abandon the conviction of Galileo that somehow, by some means, there is a movement that takes place".[24]

"What is the argument on the other side? Only this, that no case has been found in which it has been done before. That argument does not appeal to me in the least. If we never do anything which has not been done before, we shall never get anywhere. The law will stand still while the rest of the world goes on, and that will be bad for both;"

and again.[25]

"This argument about the novelty of the action does not appeal to me in the least. It has been put forward in all the great cases which have been milestones of progress in our law, and it has always, or nearly always, been rejected. If you read the great cases of *Ashby* v *White* (1703) 2 Ld. Raym. 938, *Pasley* v *Freeman* (1789) 3 Term Rep. 51 and *Donoghue* v *Stevenson* [1932] A.C. 562 you will find that in each of them the judges were divided in opinion. On the one side there were the timorous souls who were fearful of allowing a new cause of action. On the other side there were the bold spirits who were ready to allow

---

[23] *Fitzpatrick* v *Sterling Housing Association Ltd.* (C.A.) [1998] Ch. 304 per Waite L.J. @ 308.
[24] *Lister* v *Romford Ice & Storage* [1957] AC 555 per Lord Radcliffe @ 591–592.
[25] *Parker* v *Parker* [1953] 2 All ER 127 per Denning LJ @ 129.

it if justice so required. It was fortunate for the common law that the progressive view prevailed. Whenever this argument of novelty is put forward I call to mind the emphatic answer given by Pratt, C.J., nearly two hundred years ago in *Chapman v Pickersgill* (1762) 2 Wilson 145, 146 when he said: "I wish never to hear this objection again. This action is for a tort: torts are infinitely various; not limited or confined, for there is nothing in nature but may be an instrument of mischief". The same answer was given by Lord Macmillan in *Donoghue v Stevenson* [1932] A.C. 562, 619 when he said: "The criterion of judgment must adjust and adapt itself to the changing circumstances of life. The categories of negligence are never closed". I beg leave to quote those cases and those passages against those who would emphasise the paramount importance of certainty at the expense of justice. It needs only a little imagination to see how much the common law would have suffered if those decisions had gone the other way"[26]

"The common law is a developing entity as the judges develop it, and so long as we follow the well tried method of moving forward in accordance with principle as fresh facts emerge and changes in society occur, we are surely doing what Parliament intends we should do."[27]

Some senior judges are conscious of their place in history and use their judicial opinions to spark debate, to advance argument in a particular direction, or make a contribution to the body of law which they hope will endure and last. For them every word has an appropriate place and some special significance. In analysing their judgments it is your task to identify and appraise that significance.

---

[26] *Candler v Crane Christmas & Co* [1951] 2 KB 164 per Denning LJ @ 178.
[27] *Herrington v British Railways Board* [1972] AC 877 per Lord Wilberforce @ 921.

4.6

DEALING WITH TECHNICAL AND SPECIALIST VOCABULARY

Every field of knowledge has its own technical vocabulary.[28] Practitioners dealing with specialist subject matter such as construction, shipping, tax, company law, media law or clinical negligence have to cope not only with the vocabulary of the law but also the vocabulary of the field of expertise that is the subject matter of the judgment. In analysing a judgment in a technical or scientific area you may find it helpful to apply the following technique.

- Identify what kind of legal problem it is before worrying about the technical vocabulary;

- Divide the problem into its major parts;

- Separate the technical vocabulary from the ordinary words;

- Use title, section headings and preparatory remarks to clarify the position.

In doing so you will find that:

- If you have some acquaintance with the field you will recognise well-established technical vocabulary. If not you can locate the important words negatively by knowing what words must be technical, because they are not ordinary;

- Contextual analysis is here of significance: you can discover the meaning of a word you do not understand by using the meanings of all the other words you do understand in the context.

The courts are required to keep pace with technological developments and adapt their language accordingly. Often it is such developments which are at the forefront of new policy or ethical decision-making, for example in human fertilisation and embryology, where the House of Lords recently had to

---

[28] See *Adler* op.cit. p. 104.

grapple with the statutory definition of the words "live human embryo where fertilisation is complete"[29] taking in the advances made in that field since the passing of the Act:

> "My Lords, section 1 (1) of the Human Fertilisation and Embryology Act 1990 defines the scope of the regulatory system created by the Act. It provides:
>
>> "except where otherwise stated–(a) embryo means a live human embryo where fertilisation is complete, and (b) references to an embryo include an egg in the process of fertilisation, and, for this purpose, fertilisation is not complete until the appearance of a two cell zygote."
>
> In so legislating Parliament acted on the scientific insight of a decade ago, viz that an embryo could only be created by fertilisation. The ordinary and obvious meaning of section 1(1) reflects that understanding. Since 1990 the development of cell nuclear replacement has made possible the creation of an embryo without the means of fertilisation. The question arose whether embryos created by cell nuclear replacement were covered by the 1990 Act.

> **22** That leads to the question whether it is appropriate to construe the 1990 Act in the light of the new scientific knowledge. In the case law two contradictory approaches are to be found. It reminds one of the old saying that rules of interpretation "hunt in pairs": that for every rule there is a rule to the contrary effect: see *Burrows, Statute Law,* 3rd ed (2003), p 277 and chapter 12 generally. In the older cases the view often prevailed that a statute must be construed as if one were interpreting it on the day after it was passed: *The Longford* (1889) 14 PD 34, 36. This doctrine was dignified by the Latin expression contemporanea expositio est optima et fortissima in lege. But even in older cases a different approach sometimes prevailed. It was the idea encapsulated by Lord Thring, the great Victorian draftsman, that statutes ought generally to be construed as "always speaking statutes". In the Court of Appeal, Lord Phillips of Worth Matravers MR cited the early illustration of *Attorney General v Edison Telephone Co of London Ltd* (1880) 6 QBD 244. The Telegraph Act 1869 (32 & 33 Vict c 73) gave the Postmaster-General an exclusive right of transmitting telegrams. Telegrams

---

[29] Ss1(1),3(3)(3)(d) The Human Fertilisation and Embryology Act 1990. *R.(Quintavalle)* v *Secretary of State for Health* [2003] UKHL 13;[2003] 2 AC 687.

were defined as messages transmitted by telegraph. A telegraph was defined to include "any apparatus for transmitting messages or other communications by means of electric signals". When the Act was passed the only such means of communication was the process of interrupting and re-establishing electric current, thereby causing a series of clicks which conveyed information by morse code. Then the telephone was invented. It conveyed the human voice by wire by means of a new process. It was argued that because this process was unknown when the Act was passed, it could not apply to it. The court held, at p 255, that "absurd consequences would follow if the nature and extent of those powers and duties [under the Act] were made dependent upon the means employed for the purpose of giving the information"......

24 The critical question is how the court should approach the question whether, in the light of a new scientific development, the Parliamentary intent covers the new state of affairs. In a dissenting judgment in *Royal College of Nursing of the United Kingdom* v *Department of Health and Social Security* [1981] AC 800 Lord Wilberforce analysed the position with great clarity. He observed, at p 822:

"In interpreting an Act of Parliament it is proper, and indeed necessary, to have regard to the state of affairs existing, and known by Parliament to be existing, at the time. It is a fair presumption that Parliament's policy or intention is directed to that state of affairs. Leaving aside cases of omission by inadvertence, this being not such a case, when a new state of affairs, or a fresh set of facts bearing on policy, comes into existence, the courts have to consider whether they fall within the parliamentary intention. *They may be held to do so, if they fall within the same genus of facts as those to which the expressed policy has been formulated. They may also be held to do so if there can be detected a clear purpose in the legislation which can only be fulfilled if the extension is made.* How liberally these principles may be applied must depend upon the nature of the enactment, and the strictness or otherwise of the words in which it has been expressed...[30]

---

[30] *R.(Quintavalle)* v *Secretary of State for Health* [2003] UKHL 13;[2003] 2 AC 687 per Lord Steyn @ 700 [21],[22]-[25].

4.7

THE RESIDUAL USE OF LEGAL LATIN AND FRENCH

It says much for the retentive historical character of legal language that nearly a millennium after the Norman invasion we still employ both the Law-French terminology drawn from the dialect used in all legal documents and judicial proceedings from the time of William the Conqueror up to the reign of Edward III, and the odd smattering of Anglo-Saxon, such as *moot, Lammas* and *Lady Day*. Technically these words have not yet fallen foul of the most recent judicial disapproval of Latin maxims, and many have passed into the vernacular of ordinary English usage: *appeal, counsel, demand, heir, lay, merger, party, process, suit* and *mortgage*. It is hard to envisage the Chancery Bar coping without *mesne, seisin, profit-à-prendre, cestui que trust, cy-près, replevin* or *chose in action*; or the Criminal Bar without such basic words as *arrest, assault, verdict,* and *jury*, let alone *autrefois acquit / convict* and *voire dire*; for common law practitioners there are such terms of art as *lien, misfeasance, malfeasance* and *puisne*.

Since the official language of England until 1362 was French, it is hardly surprising that there is such a substantial residue of words in our day to day affairs rooted in the professional language of that era. Nearing the end of his reign, as part of the statute[31] in which English replaced French as the national language, Edward III enacted that all pleas should be pleaded and adjudged in English, but be entered and enrolled in Latin. Records of the courts continued to be entered in Latin until 25th March 1733. That was the date specified in an act of 1731[32] from and after which:

> "all writs, process and returns thereof, and proceedings thereon, and all pleadings, rules, orders, indictments, informations, inquisitions, presentments, verdicts, prohibitions, certificates, and all patents, charters, pardons, commissions, records, *judgments*, statutes, recognizances, bonds, rolls, entries, fines and recoveries, and all proceedings thereunto, and all proceedings ... whatsoever in any courts of justice

---

[31] 36 Edw III st 1 ch 15.
[32] Geo 2 c 26.

within that part of Great Britain called England, and in the Court of Exchequer in Scotland, and which concern the law and administration of justice, shall be in the English tongue and language only, and not in Latin of French, or any other tongue or language whatsoever, and shall be written in such a common legible hand and character, as the acts of parliament are usually ingrossed in, and the lines and words of the same to be written at least as close as the said acts usually are, and not in any hand commonly called court hand, and in words at length and not abbreviated; any law, custom or usage heretofore to the contrary thereof notwithstanding; and all and every person or persons offending against this act, shall for every such offence forfeit and pay the sum of fifty pounds to any person who shall sue for the same by action of debt, bill, plaint or information in any of his Majesty's courts of record in Westminster hall,..."

The position was clarified in 1733[33] to exclude the English Court of Exchequer whose "under officers, deputies and clerks, shall carry on the business to them severally and respectively belonging and appertaining, according to the usual course and antient method and practice, and in like manner as if the said act had never been made..."

So passed out of the usage of the court judgments made entirely in Latin or French, and left merely their vestigial remains in the form of maxims and terminology, the use of which remain under debate. That debate has been going on for a long time, even in the modern era. So, for example in 1943 Lord Justice du Parcq opined

"I think the cases are comparatively few in which much light is obtained by the liberal use of Latin phrases ...Nobody can derive any assistance from the phrase *novus actus interveniens* until it is translated into English"[34]

We have noted that the specialised language of the law is highly developed and remarkably variable. In meeting the demands of modern society the framers of the Civil Procedure Rules 1998 suggest that tradition alone is not sufficient reason for retaining outmoded forms of language; that lawyers and judges should use ordinary language when possible. Practitioners must learn the language of the law but wield it carefully, never losing the idiomatic flavour of the vernacular. In particular unnecessary Latinisms should be avoided to make the law more comprehensible and less intimidating to lay people.

---

[33] 6 Geo 2 c.14.
[34] *Ingram v United Automobile Services Ltd* [1943] 2 All ER 71.

The traditionalists point out that the translation of Latin maxims is unsatisfactory, leading to imprecision and lack of uniformity (e.g. *res inter alios acta*),
lengthy and convoluted alternatives (*amicus curiae*; *habeus corpus*), and in
some cases it is virtually impossible to do so without altering the intended
meaning (*de bene esse*).

Maxims tend to be tags for principles which have been developed over
centuries and are used for convenience and the speed of an interchange which
does not require explanation. Examples of this abound:

> "The doctrine of res judicata rests on the twin principles which
> cannot be better expressed than in terms of the two Latin maxims
> "interest reipublicae ut sit finis litium" and "nemo debet bis vexari
> pro una et eadem causa." These principles are of such fundamental
> importance that they cannot be confined in their application to liti-
> gation in the private law field."[35]

> "I come now to the two defences which lie at the heart of this appeal.
> They are expressed, for convenience, in two Latin maxims, *volenti non
> fit injuria and ex turpi causa non oritur actio.*"[36]

> "Of course an employer may be himself in fault by engaging an
> incompetent servant or not having a proper system of work or in
> some other way. But there is nothing of that kind in this case.
> Denning L.J. appears to base his reasoning on a literal application of
> the maxim qui facit per alium facit per se but, in my view, it is rarely
> profitable and often misleading to use Latin maxims in that way. It is
> a rule of law that an employer, though guilty of no fault himself, is
> liable for damage done by the fault or negligence of his servant acting
> in the course of his employment. The maxims respondeat superior
> and qui facit per alium facit per se are often used but I do not think
> that they add anything or that they lead to any different results. The
> former merely states the rule baldly in two words, and the latter
> merely gives a fictional explanation of it."[37]

John Gray, in his excellent study *Lawyers Latin: A Vade Mecum*[38] contends that
a change to a label serves no practical purpose. Latin expressions will continue
to be found not only in textbooks, old statutes, academic articles and judgments prior to 1999, but also in the present and future decisions of the

---

[35] *Thrasyvoulou v Secretary of State for the Environment* [1990] 2 A.C. 273 (H.L.(E.)) per Lord Bridge of
Harwich @ 289.
[36] *Kirkham v Chief Constable of Manchester* [1990] 2 Q.B. 283 (C.A.) per Lloyd L.J.@ 289.
[37] *Staveley Iron & Chemical Co. Ltd. v Jones.* [1956] 2 W.L.R. 479 (H.L.(E.)) per Lord Reid @ 486.
[38] Robert Hale, London 2002.

European Court of Justice and the European Court of Human Rights, the judges of which institutions have no similar qualms to those of Lord Woolf LCJ or Lord Irvine of Lairg LC in having Latin remain. There is no similar stricture upon the use of words derived from Law French, and the intention to modernise or simplify legal language is likely to result in no more than a mish-mash of confusion and individuality in which although most judges will no doubt comply with this part of the policy underpinning the Civil Procedure Rules, some are plainly happy to continue the use of Latin maxims where they feel it appropriate to the situation.

It is important, certainly in my own view, to recognise the distinction between terms of art for which no ordinary English equivalent exists, and those terms that are merely vestigial Latinisms with simple English substitutes:[39] a lawyers' Latin, unknown to Latin grammarians. Among the former are words used commonly by lawyers which have spilled over into ordinary and acceptable English usage: *bona fide; versus; alibi; quorum; habeus corpus; prima facie; ex parte; de minimis; ultra* or *intra vires*. It is not sensible to deliberately strip out such terms from a judgment for the sake of doing so. On the other hand pompous and bombastic expressions introduced to give an inflated sense of erudition, for example *sub suo periculo* (at his own risk), or *ex abundanti cautela* (out of abundant caution), serve no purpose and convey no special legal meaning. These have no place outside El Vinos.

On April 4th 2000 the Times Law Reports summarised the Court of Appeal judgment of 15th March in the case of *Fryer* v *Pearson* under the headnote

> "Practice – Judicial disapproval of Latin Maxims". It was reported that when concurring with Lord Justice Roch and Lord Justice Waller in dismissing the appeal, Lord Justice May observed, "People should stop using maxims or doctrines dressed up in Latin, such as "res ipsa loquitur", which are not readily comprehensible to those for whose benefit they are supposed to exist."

Of course such judicial sentiment was *obiter dictum*.

---

[39] See *A Dictionary of Modern Legal Usage* Bryan A. Garner OUP New York 1987.

4.8
LITERARY STYLE IN JUDGMENTS

In continental systems professional judges are trained in writing judgments in a uniform manner. The form and language are expected to conceal individualistic styles. In Britain judges are almost entirely free to choose both the form and language of their opinions. They can be idiosyncratic, even slightly rebellious: at least two of the judges who contributed to this book said that ever since the disapproval of the continued use of legal Latin they have endeavoured to ensure that at least one Latin phrase is to be found in every judgment of theirs. Such freedom means that judicial style is infinitely varied.

The development of the written reserved judgment has highlighted the drawbacks of the oral tradition in terms of style. Commonly transcripts of judgments delivered *ex tempore* show hesitation, repetition, filler phrases, and sentences without proper punctuation, grammar, syntax or verbs, as well as pomposity and overblown phrases. By contrast judges consider with great care the use of the written word and often its literary effect. They can polish and re-polish, moderate their position, set out facts and arguments more fully, yet make the whole judgment shorter. You should admire such carefully prepared, written compositions for their mannered prose, reflection and craft.

Judges of the superior courts take considerable care when preparing reserved judgments. They either have or make the time to reflect on the language that they will use, often mulling over the choice of individual words to be precise about what they wish to say. Even in a fairly uncomplicated case it can be a huge piece of work, and will invariably take at least a day. The superior the court, the more precise and highly focussed is the use of language.

Even at first instance, judges writing what can be a lengthy piece of prose either deliberately consider or subconsciously use literary techniques to order their thoughts, to emphasise their reasoning, and to persuade the reader of the legitimacy of their views.

We have considered the more sophisticated use of form and structure in contemporary judgments, which give rise to sub-headings, numbered paragraphs and rhetorical questions (see Part 3.3 above). Let us now turn to consider the impact of individual literary style used by judges to convey their decisions and their argument.

The modern judge is as individual a literary stylist as any of his predecessors, but his audience has changed as society has undoubtedly become less lettered, perhaps less educated generally (and undoubtedly starved of historical and literary references), and certainly more culturally diverse since the 1960s. Most first instance judges feel that litigants need to hear judgments in clear and simple language: short words, short sentences and plain English wherever possible, particularly in family cases. This translates on the written page as short paragraphs, and a conscious absence of the repetition of words unless absolutely necessary. A cross between Lord Denning and a *Sun* leader, as one civil recorder put it.

While they will conscientiously avoid the use of clichés, jargon, catch phrases and pure slang, there is an increasing tendency for judges in the lower courts to use colloquialism, with or without quotation marks, but particularly phrases drawn from the witnesses' own evidence. Swear words in primary evidence are mostly edited out as a matter of taste and decency. The majority of judges questioned at all levels, but by no means all, favoured the use of analogy, especially its effect in *reductio in absurdum* as a useful device in reality testing. However the intentional use of simile and metaphor seems presently to be out of favour. Synonyms are commonly used to avoid the repetition of words.

Administrative tribunals tend to use everyday language since their decisions are usually formed with the consensus of the lay members and directed at the parties themselves. They tend to use a more conversational style. For chairmen it is important to write in good clear plain English and to distinguish between language having a legal and a non-legal meaning, and deliberately to avoid modern colloquialism and slang expressions unless directly referable to the evidence.

In the higher courts reserved judgments are far more polished. Language remains formal, and literary style is considered important. This is not so much to make the writing complex and give judges the opportunity to deliver passages of purple prose, but to devise as elegant a structure and style as is in keeping with the importance and gravitas of the work being undertaken. For some judges elegance of style is seen as the key to having their judgments readily remembered and made easy to cite. Whatever may be said against over-flowery language, purple passages attract attention – of the media and lay readers as well as practitioners.

Most judges are not conscious of the longevity of their decisions: at first instance a judgment will normally be so fact-sensitive that its lifespan will extend only to the remedy given to the winning party or any appeal. In the higher tribunals both the courts and practitioners currently seem to be obsessed with only what is recent, and will happily pass over distinguished authority that is a mere 10 years old. Even the most senior judges do not write for posterity, should they wish to do so; their opinions concerning the most important of cases have a sense of immediacy and practicality which tries to take account of the extraordinary pace of political, social and economic change which afflicts our present generation of lawyers.

4.9

JUDICIAL LITERARY TECHNIQUES

Whatever techniques are being used to compel the attention of the reader to the force of the argument, they have to be applicable in practice to the particular situation in that case. However attractive the composition of a judgment, the argument must be of practical effect as well as sound conclusion. As a piece of prose it may read beautifully, but a judicial opinion must be both workable as well as intelligible and intellectually satisfying. Having said that you will find upon an analytical reading the following common techniques that are used on a frequent basis to give a literary patina to the discerning reader of what are both well-remembered judgments and good prose.

IMPERATIVE AND DECLARATIVE SENTENCES

The declarative sentence sets out the proposition being advanced. The imperative adds emphasis. Both use examples to show how principles work in practice. You are more familiar with this than any other method since, from an analytical point of view, this is the mechanism by which the doctrine of precedent operates: the more appropriate the example, the more persuasive the argument.

THE COMPRESSIVE METAPHOR

This is the familiar thought-provoking axiom that encapsulates in one sentence a whole legal tradition. To take two American examples,

> *"danger invites rescue. The cry of distress is the summons to relief...The risk of rescue, if only it be not wanton, is born of the occasion. The emergency begets the man,"*[40] and

> *"The soundness of a conclusion may not infrequently be tested by its consequences;"*[41]

---

[40] *Wagner* v *International Railway* (1921) 244 NY 176; 155 N.E. 58 Cardozo.
[41] *Ostrowe* v *Lee* (1931) 256 NY 36; 175 NE 505.

and some closer to home:

> *"justice is only blind or blindfolded to the extent necessary to hold its scales evenly. It is not, and must never be allowed, to become blind to the reality of the situation, lamentable though that situation may be."*[42]

> *"If common error can make the law, so can parliamentary error."*[43]

THE ELEGANT VARIATION

Judges will often, although cautiously, use synonyms following the general literary guidance, "the repetition of a single word over and over is awkward and boring, so good writers often substitute different words having the same or very similar meanings for important words in their text."[44]

This is, of course, dangerous in a situation where precision is more important than literary style. Slight changes in meaning may become very important and lead to variations in construction. The judge can change his vocabulary but must take care not to change the legal terminology.

THE FACTUAL ALLUSION

The most common technique in reasoning is to import an example, akin to the factual situation, but either simplified or made more extreme to demonstrate the logic of or the flaw in the argument. Commonly judges use letters to replace names in such examples:

> "We agree that the authorities establish that actual knowledge or reckless indifference is (in shorthand) the test for the dishonest state of mind on each point. But in every case it will be necessary to look carefully at the facts in order to apply the test. Suppose that A, a civil servant, accepts a bribe from B for causing either his (B's) or some other person's (C's) name and address to be improperly deleted from, or added to, an official database. The consequences of such improper action might range from B obtaining some grant or subsidy to which he was not entitled, to some third party, C, being harassed by official demands which ought not to have been made. A may be either a young and inexperienced clerk, or an experienced officer in a respon-

---

[42] *Attorney-General* v *Guardian Newspapers (No.2)* [1990] 1 AC 109 CA per Sir John Donaldson MR @ 197.
[43] *Lowsley* v *Forbes* [1999] 1 AC 329 per Lord Lloyd of Berwick @ 342.
[44] *Adler* op.cit. p. 127.

sible managerial position. In either case A would be hard put to contend that taking a bribe was not dishonest (and that would, of course, give rise to criminal liability). But whether A knew of, or was recklessly indifferent to, injury to C so as to incur civil liability to C would depend on all circumstances. That would be so whether the claim was against A personally or was against the government department where A worked."[45]

THE LITERARY ALLUSION

Judges are not shy of using quotations from literature or the bible to illustrate a point. Lord Coleridge CJ cited Milton as an authority against the defence arguments in the famous case of *R* v *Dudley & Stephens*.[46] In *Miller* v *David* [47] he cites Dr Johnson. In the present day Lord Millett managed to cite the Book of Common Prayer, W.S.Gilbert, and Milton in the same paragraph:[48]

> The words "dwell" and "dwelling" are not terms of art with a specialised legal meaning. They are ordinary English words, even if they are perhaps no longer in common use. They mean the same as "inhabit" and "habitation" or more precisely "abide" and "abode", and refer to the place where one lives and makes one's home. They suggest a greater degree of settled occupation than "reside" and "residence", connoting the place where the occupier habitually sleeps and usually eats, but the idea that he must also cook his meals there is found only in the law reports. It finds no support in English literature. According to the Book of Common Prayer, "the fir trees are a dwelling for the storks" (Psalm 104); while W S Gilbert condemned the billiard sharp "to dwell in a dungeon cell" (where it will be remembered he plays with a twisted cue on a cloth untrue with elliptical billiard balls): The Mikado, Act II. It is hardly necessary to observe that Victorian prison cells did not possess cooking facilities. Of course, the word "dwell" may owe its presence to the exigencies of the rhyme, but it does not strike the listener as incongruous. If faintly humorous, it is because the occupation of a prison cell is involuntary, not because of the absence of cooking facilities. As I shall show hereafter, Gilbert, who had qualified at the Bar, had got his law right. An earlier and greater poet wrote of Lucifer being hurled "to bottomless perdition, there to dwell in adamantine chaos and penal fire": (*Paradise Lost* Book I, l 47).

---

[45] Per Hirst LJ in *Three Rivers District Council* v *Bank of England (No. 3)* [2003] 2 AC @ 54.
[46] (1884) 14 QBD 273 @ 288.
[47] (1874) LR 9 CP 118 @ 125.
[48] *Uratemp Ventures Ltd* v *Collins* [2002] 1 AC 301 @ 310.

Lord Hailsham was equally fond of both Gilbert and *The Mikado*:

> "The prosecution authorities have had no such qualms as I feel. They have pursued the matter from the magistrates to the Divisional Court, from the Divisional Court to the House of Lords. Their argument is agreeable and compact. The Act says nothing about fraud. It says nothing about intent. It says nothing to the effect that the defendant must at least know at the moment at which the false statement was made that it was being made in a form which was different from that which was then intended. It simply says that at the moment at which the statement is made the defendant must know that the statement was false. At first sight the appellant's argument was that anticipated by W. S. Gilbert in *The Mikado*:
>
> > "Mikado: That's the pathetic part of it. Unfortunately the fool of an Act says: 'compassing the death of the Heir Apparent.' There's not a word about a mistake.' – At this stage I must enter a caveat: wait and see.
> >
> > "Koko, Pitti-sing and Nanki Poo: No.
> >
> > "Mikado: Or not knowing." But see above.
> >
> > "Koko: No.
> >
> > "Mikado: Or having no notion.
> >
> > "Pitti-Sing: No.
> >
> > "Mikado: Or not being there.
> >
> > "Nanki Poo: No.
> >
> > "Mikado: There should be of course.
> >
> > "Koko, Pitti-sing and Nanki Poo: Yes.
> >
> > "Mikado: But there isn't.
> >
> > "Koko, Pitti-sing and Nanki Poo: Oh.
> >
> > "Mikado: That is the slovenly way in which these Acts are always drawn."

Unfortunately for the respondents, the last remark of the Mikado is not fair to the Trade Descriptions Act 1968. In that Act, there are words about mistake and having no notion. These words are to be found in section 24 which I have set out above in extenso, and if they are successfully invoked they provide an avenue of escape for the defendant who has acted innocently. This section provides a special defence which is available to a defendant in section 14 cases. But this defence has two characteristics. It must be expressly invoked by prior notice (section 24(2)), and the burden of proof is on the defendant (section 24(1)), though presumably on the balance of probabilities. The respondents altogether failed to invoke this section and have therefore to rely solely on the words of section 14(1)(a) which, in their literal sense are not favourable to this construction. This, I fear, is fatal to the respondents' chances of succeeding in this appeal".[49]

The modern judiciary favour wider literary allusions, for example, to Charles Lamb:

"It is also common ground that the public with whom we are concerned for the purposes of the subsection as consumers or users (and we do not think that there is any real distinction to be drawn between these two terms in this case) consists of individual retail buyers of books for their own reading, readers of books in public and institutional libraries, borrowers of books from all kinds of lending libraries and, no doubt, that class of borrowers also which Charles Lamb (Charles Lamb, Essays of Elia and Eliana (1882), E. Moxon Son & Co., London; The Two Races of Men, p. 39.) denounced as mutilators of collections, spoilers of the symmetry of shelves and creators of odd volumes, the borrowers from private persons, as well as the recipients of books given as presents. We do not think, however, that for the purposes of this judgment we need distinguish the last two classes from the lenders or donors: we can regard their interests as the same as those of people who buy for their own reading".[50]

and to Jeremy Bentham,

16 The starting point must be the importance of the principle of open justice. This has been a thread to be discerned throughout the common law systems: "Publicity is the very soul of justice. It is the keenest spur to exertion, and the surest of all guards against improbity. It keeps the judge himself, while trying, under trial": see Benthamiana, or Select Extracts from the Works of Jeremy Bentham (1843), p 115.[51]

---

[49] Wings v Ellis [1985] AC 272 HL @ 289.
[50] In Re Net Book Agreement 1957 [1962] 1 WLR 1347 per Buckley J @ 1375.
[51] Clibbery v Allan [2002] Fam 270 per Dame Butler-Sloss P @ [16].

and of course, to Shakespeare:

> "We find this usage in Shakespeare, *Othello:* Act III, scene IV: where Othello says to Desdemona:
>
>> "That handkerchief
>> Did an Egyptian to my mother give.
>> She was a charmer, and could almost read
>> The thoughts of people."[52]

The use of literary reference also appears to be well-developed in the European tradition:

> '**17** Although it is true that *Sieckmann* concerned olfactory trade marks, the considerations which I set out concerning odours are applicable to messages received by hearing. The Court of Justice itself so stated in its judgment, when it ruled that article 2 of the Directive allows signs not capable of being perceived visually to constitute a trade mark: see p 508, para 42, and p 512, first paragraph of the oper-ative part. The ability of sounds and, in particular, music to identify derives from its evocative intensity, which converts sounds into a specific language. Marcel Proust was able to capture it in a decisive passage in *In search of lost time*, where the narrator asks
>
>> "whether music is not the only example of what – had language, the formation of words, the analysis of ideas, not been invented – might have been the communication between souls. It is a possi-bility which was not subsequently developed; humanity followed other routes, the way of spoken and written expression": Marcel Proust, *A la Recherche du Temps Perdu, La Prisonnière*, ed Gallimard (La Pléiade), Paris (1988), vol III, pp 762 and 763.
>
> That idea is based on the philosophy of Schopenhauer, expressed in his work *The World as Will and Representation*, in which he assigns to music the same revelatory and transcendent function as that subse-quently attributed to it by Proust's work, avoiding the poetic explana-tions and with the same attention to time: *Arthur Schopenhauer, Le Monde Comme Volonté et Comme Représentation*, ed PUF, translated by A Burdeau (1888), revised and corrected by R Roos, Paris (1966), p 340. In short, Proust literally paraphrased Schopenhauer's text, in particular, in relation to the capacity of music to interpret the intimate essence of things (Anne Henry, *Marcel Proust, Théories pour*

---

[52] *Commission for Racial Equality* v *Dutton* [1989] QB 783 CA per Nicholls LJ @ 796.

une esthétique, ed Klienchsieck, Paris (1981), p 303), since the novel relies on a metaphysical aesthetic from which it translates the abstract and theoretical content into the attitudes experienced, into the actions, into the sentiments which constitute the substance of an artistic work (*Jean-Jacques Nattiez, Proust musicien*, ed Christian Bourgois, Paris (1975), p 162), taking into account above all that music imitates life and prefigures the work on which the novelist must embark in order to combine the strands in a single and organised whole, since he functions as the involuntary memory: the reappearance of a melody already heard brings to mind the first hearing, as the flagstones of the pavement, in Proust's work, bring to the narrator's mind the episode of the Madeleine: J J Nattiez, op cit, p 121.'[53]

SIMPLIFICATION OF IDEAS

Like the factual allusion, judges create memorable passages by illustrating an important point with a commonplace example. If you remember the example, it acts as a reminder of the doctrine or principle. Over the past decade Lord Hoffmann created an enduring image when dealing with causation in professional negligence:

"Rules which make the wrongdoer liable for all the consequences of his wrongful conduct are exceptional and need to be justified by some special policy. Normally the law limits liability to those consequences which are attributable to that which made the act wrongful. In the case of liability in negligence for providing inaccurate information, this would mean liability for the consequences of the information being inaccurate.

I can illustrate the difference between the ordinary principle and that adopted by the Court of Appeal by an example. A mountaineer about to undertake a difficult climb is concerned about the fitness of his knee. He goes to a doctor who negligently makes a superficial examination and pronounces the knee fit. The climber goes on the expedition, which he would not have undertaken if the doctor had told him the true state of his knee. He suffers an injury which is an entirely foreseeable consequence of mountaineering but has nothing to do with his knee.

---

[53] *Shield Mark BV v Kist* [2004] Ch 101 ECJ per Advocate General Colomer @ 102 [17].

On the Court of Appeal's principle, the doctor is responsible for the injury suffered by the mountaineer because it is damage which would not have occurred if he had been given correct information about his knee. He would not have gone on the expedition and would have suffered no injury. On what I have suggested is the more usual principle, the doctor is not liable. The injury has not been caused by the doctor's bad advice because it would have occurred even if the advice had been correct."[54]

OTHER TECHNIQUES

- Varying the lengths of paragraphs to keep the reader's interest.

- Keeping paragraphs short: this enables the judge to identify one idea or topic, or one illustration. This brings clarity to the structure and separates out the point being made while at the same time gives momentum to the piece of writing as a whole.

---

[54] *South Australian Asset Management Corporation v York Montague Ltd* [On appeal from *Banque Bruxelles Lambert S.A.* v *Eagle Star Insurance Co. Ltd.*] [1997] AC 191 @ 213.

4.10
THE IMPACT OF DISTINCTIVE JUDICIAL LITERARY STYLE

How you appraise judicial style may be a matter of personal taste and reaction. But commentators[55] have posed the questions does a particular literary style make a judgment more compelling? Does the language of a judgment give it a greater influence, both contemporaneously and afterwards historically, than it merits? The age of formal rhetoric within judgments may have passed, but much can be learned from those giants of juristic style, Benjamin Cardozo, Justice of the Supreme Court of the United States 1932–1938, Sir Owen Dixon, Chief Justice of Australia 1952–1964 and Lord Denning, Lord of Appeal in Ordinary from 1957 and Master of the Rolls 1962–1982. Each judge still retains an immense following, respect and affection among both practitioners and fellow judges in both their own jurisdictions and beyond.

Much of their reputation concerns not the substance of their opinions, but the way in which these were expressed. They imbued their writing with an apparent simplicity by the use of a succession of short sentences formed into staccato paragraphs. This gave their judgments both fluidity and the appearance of decisiveness. Both laymen and lawyer could read these with equal interest, although not necessarily with the same intellectual satisfaction. Such judicial opinion demonstrated the idea that good style may impress practitioners because it makes judgments more readily memorable. This is a common thread in the opinions of both Justice Cardozo and Lord Denning.

Benjamin Cardozo was a great believer in literary embellishments as devices to help persuade. He thought that clarity of itself may not be enough to give persuasive force to an opinion, and used such devices as alliteration, antithesis, proverbs and maxims. He varied his sentences to make his points

---

[55] See in particular the footnotes to and sources given in *The Form and Language of Judicial Opinions* (2002) 118 LQR 226 by Lord Rodger of Earlsferry from which I have drawn heavily in the preparation of this section.

either terse or sincere.[56] The foundation for his view is curious, as explained by Lord Roger in *The Form and Language of Judicial Opinions*:[57]

> "he thought of an opinion as having to "win its way". In other words, he saw his opinions as being in a competitive struggle with other opinions on the same topic. That would, I think, be natural for a judge in the United States with a vast number of individual State systems and, at the time when he wrote, a federal system of common law. The law reporting system was well established and so lawyers and judges had ready access to competing decisions from all over the country. In that situation Cardozo rightly saw that, if attractive or some how arresting, the style in which he wrote might make his opinion, and hence the doctrine which it contained, more persuasive to courts and practitioners. And in this he was not wrong. Cardozo's opinions continue to be among those most cited in America to this day."[58]

Sir Owen Dixon (1886–1972) who was an immensely distinguished Australian jurist, and famous for his interpretations of the Australian constitution, who presided over the legal system of the Australian Commonwealth at a time when there was a tension between following English law and creating a domestic law influenced more by the American model. His judgments have been cited with approval or followed in over 60 cases reported in the Law Reports.

The distinctiveness of Lord Denning's technique came from his narrative style constructed in short sentences which suggests to the reader he is delivering a homily; he uses an almost child-like idealism when discussing legal principles, and deliberately suppresses any overt intellectualising. His aim was always to do justice, rather than apply the law strictly, and he did not shrink from undermining established doctrine that he found inconvenient in arriving at a just solution to the problem. The simplicity of his style enabled his critics, particularly in the House of Lords, to overturn many of his decisions.

Lord Denning's style may most easily be seen by comparing it with the judgments of his brother judges when he sat. Much the best example is in *Beswick v Bewick* [1966] Ch 538 where he opens his judgment[59] thus:

---

[56] *Law and Literature* Cardozo 1925.
[57] *Op. cit.* @ 239–241.
[58] For further readings see A. L Kaufman *Cardozo* (1998), R.A.Posner *Cardozo: a Study in Reputation* (1990), R.D.Friedman *On Cardozo and Reputation: Legendary Judge, Underrated Justice?* (1991) 12 Cardozo LR 1923.
[59] @549.

"Old Peter Beswick was a coal merchant in Eccles, Lancashire. He had no business premises. All he had was a lorry, scales and weights. He used to take the lorry to the yard of the National Coal Board, where he bagged coal and took it round to his customers in the neighbourhood. His nephew, John Joseph Beswick, helped him in the business.

In March, 1962, old Peter Beswick and his wife were both over 70. He had had his leg amputated and was not in good health. The nephew was anxious to get hold of the business before the old man died. So they went to a solicitor, Mr. Ashcroft, who drew up an agreement for them. The business was to be transferred to the nephew: old Peter Beswick was to be employed in it as a consultant for the rest of his life at £6 10s. a week. After his death the nephew was to pay to his widow an annuity of £5 per week, which was to come out of the business. The agreement was quite short and I will read it in full...

...After the agreement was signed, the nephew took over the business and ran it. The old man seems to have found it difficult at first to adjust to the new situation, but he settled down. The nephew paid him £6 10s. a week. But, as expected, he did not live long. He died on November 3, 1963, leaving his widow, who was 74 years of age and in failing health. The nephew paid her the first £5. But he then stopped paying her and has refused to pay her any more.

On June 30, 1964, the widow took out letters of administration to her husband's estate. On July 15, 1964, she brought an action against the nephew for the promised £5 a week. She sued in the capacity of administratrix of the estate of Peter Beswick, deceased, and in her personal capacity she claimed £175 arrears and a declaration. By amendment she claimed specific performance and the appointment of a receiver. The action came for hearing before the Vice-Chancellor of the County Palatine of Lancaster, who held that she had no right to enforce the agreement. He dismissed the action.

If the decision of the Vice-Chancellor truly represents the law of England, it would be deplorable. It would mean that the nephew could keep the business to himself, and at the same time repudiate his promise to pay the widow. Nothing could be more unjust. I am sure the Vice-Chancellor would have decided in favour of the widow if he had not felt himself bound by the decision of Wynn-Parry J. in *In re Miller's Agreement*. That case is cited in the textbooks as if it were the last word on the subject: see Anson on Contracts, 22nd ed. (1964), p. 381; Cheshire and Fifoot on Contracts, 5th ed. (1960), p. 377. It is very like this case. So we must examine it with some care."

The third judgment in this case is given by Lord Justice Salmon, where at 563 D-G he opens the same claim in this way:

> "...the problem raised by this appeal can be stated quite simply. Under a contract between A and B, A promises that he will transfer all the assets of his business to B in consideration of a promise by B that B will pay C (a person in whom A is interested) £5 a week for the rest of C's life. A duly transfers all the assets to B, B pays one instalment to C and then refuses to make any further payments under the contract. Does the law allow B to take the full benefit of the contract and evade his contractual obligations with impunity? If so, there must be something fundamentally wrong with the law, for no system of jurisprudence should permit what is manifestly such a monstrous injustice.
>
> Throughout this judgment I will, for the sake of clarity, refer to A, B, and C. A is the late Mr. Peter Beswick and also the plaintiff standing in his shoes in her capacity as administratrix. B is the defendant and C is the plaintiff in her personal capacity."

You may think Lord Denning's famous openings contrived, but they do arrest the attention of the reader immediately, and they are, of course, truly memorable. They borrow their simplicity of language from the American tradition. The use of continuous narrative in which the facts and law are woven together to form a story is both undemanding of the reader and extremely effective. Stylistically he carries the reader forward: encouraged along his pathway you want his opinion to be right.

Lord Bingham said of his judicial opinions,

> "Lord Denning's judgments were rooted not in abstract jurisprudential principal but in the vivid experience of recognizable men and women. It was this human dimension, coupled with a distinctive literary style, which gave his judgments their unmistakeable and very personal quality."[60]

Lord Denning himself explained his own style:

> "I took infinite pains in the writing of an opinion. I crossed out sentence after sentence. I wrote them again and again. Seek to make your opinions clear at all costs. Make them positive and definite. Not neutral or vacillating. My pupil master told me early on of the client's complaint: 'I want your opinion and not your doubts', and of Sir

---

[60] Address delivered by Lord Bingham LCJ, at Westminster Abbey on 17 June 1999 at the Service of Thanksgiving for the Rt. Hon Lord Denning O.M.

George Jessel's characteristic saying: 'I may be wrong and sometimes am, but I am never in doubt.'[61]

Lord Rodger concluded[62] that the style and mannerisms of a judge's opinions may have a disproportionate influence on the way in which posterity ultimately assesses the work of that judge. This is certainly true of judges of generations past. When questioned, contemporary judges tend to come up with the same names of those whose judgments they admire: from the Victorian era Sir George Jessel MR, and Lord Justice Scrutton; from the inter-war years Lord Atkin; from the era in which our present senior judges were themselves practitioners, Lord Devlin, Lord Reid, Lord Wilberforce and Sir Robert Megarry. From the more recent past Lord Oliver, Lord Lloyd of Berwick, and among our contemporaries Lord Bingham, Lord Millett, Lord Hoffmann, Lord Steyn, Lady Hale, Lady Butler-Sloss and Lord Robert Walker. From the Scots courts Lord Watson;[63] and, from the United States, Oliver Wendel Holmes.[64]

It is fair to say that judges take a reasonably common view of those in the past whose judgments they regard as difficult, obtuse and stylistically turgid. Notwithstanding his intellect and dominance of the Appellate and Judicial Committees of his time, Lord Diplock appears to be now so regarded, and Lord Evershed before him.

Of course tastes and style may change as generations of younger lawyers come to the bench at a time when not only social values but the very approach to language and its use may be different. The present generation of practitioners will come increasingly under the influence, if not the dominance of European ideas and tradition. Over the past thirty years there has been substantially increased international contacts among the judiciary. Senior jurists who formerly practised in other jurisdictions, such as Lord Hoffman, Lord Steyn and Lord Cooke have drawn strength from it. In expressing support for their judicial opinions Lord Goff and Lord Steyn are both champions of academic work and the use of international comparative law, and this is reflected in both the substance and style of their opinions.

Even though the law may have moved on, the student of the compelling, well-constructed and well-reasoned judgment would benefit from reading for their stylistic differences the speeches of Lord Devlin in *McCutcheon* v *David McBrayne Ltd.*,[65] Lord Wilberforce in *Anns* v *Merton L.B.C.* [1978] AC 728 @ 749 and in *Ansiminic* v *Foreign Compensation Commission* [1969] 2 AC 147 @ 206,

---

[61] Lord Denning *The Discipline of Law* (Butterworths 1979) 7.
[62] *Op.cit* @ p.242.
[63] Lord of Appeal in Ordinary 1880–1899.
[64] Justice of the Supreme Court 1902–1932.
[65] [1964] 1 WLR 125@132.

Lord Lloyd of Berwick in *Marc Rich & Co* v *Bishop Rock Ltd* [1996] AC 211 @ 218 (dissenting), and in comparing the speech of Lord Goff in *White v Jones* [1995] 2 AC 207 @ 252 with the judgment of Sir Donald Nicholls V-C in the Court of Appeal.[66]

---

[66] [1995] 2 AC 207 @ 216.

PART 5
ANALYSING JUDGMENTS: REASONING, ARGUMENT AND LEGAL LOGIC

5
REASONING, ARGUMENT AND LEGAL LOGIC

"The more experienced the judge the more likely it is that he may display the virtue of brevity...the essential test is: does the judgment sufficiently explain what the judge has found and what he has concluded as well as the process of reasoning by which he has arrived at his findings, and then his conclusions?"[1]

"Precise and accurate use of ordinary language is not enough in itself to win cases. Where there is no emotional language to attract the jury, more attention must be paid to the argument. For success in advocacy, therefore, elegance of language must be supplemented by elegance of reasoning...Elegance to the Roman jurists was not a matter of words but ideas."[2]

Cases are decided by rational or objective means, but with a pragmatic, purposive approach to the facts. Judgments are based on reasoned principles, whether of general expediency, the balance of convenience, moral standards, or whatever other legitimate principles a court might have recourse to: law is or should be a rational process.[3]

Unlike the continental system, the order of precedent in the common law means that judges are not compelled to follow close patterns of logic to arrive at their conclusion, which might act as a straightjacket. Unlike the application of fixed rules, a case-by-case examination of facts does not give rise to abstract formulae, or lead to unwanted, undesirable and unjust directions in the law, even if certainty of application and the consistency of results are desirable.

In this jurisdiction, the House of Lords debated over 60 years ago the place of pure logic in the judge's approach, and concluded that consistency had to give

---

[1] *Re D* [2003] 2 FLR 1035 per Thorpe LJ @ 1040 para [11].
[2] Prof Peter Stein, *Elegance in Law* (1961) 77 LQR 242.
[3] See Dennis Lloyd *Reason and Logic in the Common Law* (1948) 64 LQR 468 for this *et seq.*

way to practical application in each case: see per Lord Wright in *Liebosch Dredger* v *Edison*[4] and Lord Macmillan[5] and Viscount Simons[6] in *Read* v *Lyons*[7] rejecting the suggestion of the Court of Appeal in *Read* that:

"though law was not logic, the nearer one could get to logic the better, and there was an inherent illogicality in the defendant's contention, which should be rejected as the plaintiff's contention made for consistency."

Lord Macmillan said in *Read*,

"Arguments based on legal consistency are apt to mislead for the common law is a practical code adapted to deal with the manifold diversities of human life."

The common lawyer will readily understand the reluctance of the court to apply a strictly logical methodology in deciding cases, logic being a method of reasoning where deductions are rigorously and necessarily inferred from general premises. The claims with which courts are concerned require the judge to make deductions from particular facts, not generalities that have to be hedged around with endless qualifications. While the law is concerned with elucidation of general propositions and their application to particular cases, courts can never construe propositions as pure generalities unrelated to the facts of life into which they must be integrated. The judge is not so much concerned with logic or reason but with 'reasonableness', which is a matter of opinion. You are conducting an exercise in assessing whether that opinion has a proper basis, and is not merely capricious or arbitrary.

At first instance the findings of fact are applied to broad, established principles to do practical justice between the parties as the court sees it. On appeal, the intervention of policy matters guides the ebb and flow of such principles in accordance with the needs of contemporary society more generally, and is not confined to the specific wishes of the parties. But for both the advocate seeking to persuade the judge, and the court to justify its decision, at each level the argument must follow a process of logical and progressive reasoning. Bentham said,[8] "Good laws are such laws for which good reasons can be given."

---

[4] [1933] AC 460.
[5] [1947] AC 160 @ 175.
[6] [1947] AC 160 @ 180.
[7] [1947] AC 160.
[8] Jeremy Bentham *Works* ix 357.

Let us start by preparing the context in which to analyse the judge's reasoning or his application of logical principles.

- Identify the scope of the dispute.

- Distinguish the material facts – find those facts in issue, the determination of which will form the basis of judge's decision: a fact is relevant if it enables the judge to conclude an issue.

- Assess their materiality by reference to the legal issues involved in the case, bearing in mind that even material facts are not of equal importance.

- Understand the relationship between the facts and the law: identify not just relevant facts, but legally relevant facts.

- Overlay the rules of evidence.

- Apply the burden of proof.

There is no essential difference between a legal argument and any other kind of argument. The principles of logic or rational thought are the same whether they be applied by lawyers or laymen. Lawyers do not possess a monopoly of the arts of demonstration, interpretation, comparison and logical analysis; though perhaps they should be able to articulate them better than most. If two doctors were to argue a moot point of their science in a public court they would set about it in much the same way as lawyers do. The cases they would cite would be patients and experiments. They would appeal to writers of authority, to common sense, to principles of natural science in general and medical science in particular. But naturally they would deal chiefly in actual cases of medical experience. This is reflected in expert evidence provided to the court. So in a legal discussion counsel are concerned chiefly with actual cases of legal experience, and very often such cases cover all the necessary ground. However it does not follow that cases and decisions are the only essential materials allowed by the lawyer in building up the structure of his argument.

As Justice Oliver Wendel Holmes put it,[9]

> "the life of the law has not been logic; it has been experience. The felt necessities of the times, the prevalent moral and political theories, intuitions of public policy, avowed or unconscious, even the prejudices which judges share with their fellow men, have had a good deal more to do than the syllogism in determining the rules by which men should be governed."

[9] Holmes *Common Law* (1881) p. 1.

FIND ?!

Coke said "the Common Law of England is the perfection of reason, gotten by long study, observation, and experience."[10]

In a system of law founded on binding precedent courts are severely limited in applying a rational process by the necessity to conform with earlier precedents. As we shall examine, there is scope for the judge to draw distinctions of fact between the case before him and earlier cases. In this sense the law reduces itself to the art of drawing distinctions, and in the case of the practitioner, anticipating the distinctions the judge is likely to draw: for present purposes we must consider whether the judge was correct in drawing a particular distinction since such distinctions may often be in the nature of hair-splitting, this being the only method to hand for avoiding the consequences of an earlier decision which the court considers unreasonable or as laying down a principle which is not to be extended.

Start then, by assuming that the judge has based his own argument on a process that is both rational and of practical application in the sense that his intended result has a practical effect. Examine the judge's reasoning in stages: the judgment is a path along which to proceed empirically and gradually, testing the ground at each step and not worrying about the absence of any broad theoretical principles or to feel any dismay or discomfort because the facts of a situation could not be moulded into any pre-established and consistent theoretical framework. It is not unlike the kind of incremental development in the law of negligence considered by Lord Bridge in *Caparo Industries* v *Dickman*.[11]

---

[10] Sir Edward Coke *Inst*.Pt.I § 138.
[11] [1990] 2 AC 605 @ 618.

5.1
LOCATING THE ARGUMENTS

Identify in the judgment the most important paragraphs and sentences. This is not a matter of length. It is a question of the relationship between language and thought. Nor is it always the case that the argument will be contained in one unit of writing.

The logical unit is a sequence of propositions, some of which give rise to further development; but it is not uniquely related to any recognizable block of writing, as terms are related to words and phrases, and propositions to sentences. An argument may be expressed in a single complicated sentence. Or it may be expressed in a number of sentences that are part only of one paragraph. Sometimes an argument may correspond with a paragraph, but it may also happen that an argument runs through several or many paragraphs.[12] Equally there are many paragraphs in any judgment that do not express an argument at all, nor even part of one. These may consist of collections of sentences that detail evidence or report how the evidence has been gathered. They are of secondary importance.

If the argument is not expressed in self-contained paragraphs it may be necessary to draw it together by taking discreet sentences from different paragraphs until a sequence can be made of all those sentences containing the propositions which form the argument. After discovering the leading sentence the construction of such a paragraph should be relatively easy.

Modern judgments tend either to have a formal summary of the argument or a paragraph or section in which the argument is recapitulated. A well-reasoned judgment usually summarises itself as its arguments develop. If the judge summarises his arguments for you at the end of a section you should be able to look back over the preceding paragraphs and find the materials he has brought together in summary. If you have undertaken an inspectional reading before beginning to read the judgment analytically, you will know whether summary passages exist and if so where they are.

---

[12] See *Adler op.cit.* p. 129.

A sign of a poorly reasoned or loosely constructed judgment is the omission of steps in an argument. Sometimes they can be omitted without damage or inconvenience because the propositions left out can generally be supplied from the common knowledge of the reader, either because the judge is aware that a party or his lawyer does not or should not require them. Sometimes the omission is misleading and occasionally intentional. One of the familiar tricks of the orator or propagandist is to leave certain things unsaid, things that are highly relevant to the argument, but that might be challenged if they were made explicit. The omission may prevent you from identifying a logical flaw. Careful reading should uncover whether every step in an argument is made explicit.

5.2
UNITS OF REASONING

Good argument in a simple case ought to be put in a nutshell. In the course of a more elaborate analysis one proposition may be established in order to prove another and this may be used in turn to build a further point. The units of reasoning are, however, single arguments. If you can find these you are not likely to miss the larger sequences. Usually an argument will involve a number of statements. Of these, some give reasons why you should accept the conclusion the judge is proposing. If you find the conclusion look for the reasons; if you find the reasons, first see where they lead.

It is trite to suggest that every line of argument must start somewhere: there are two basic starting places – an agreed assumption of fact or law, or a self-evident proposition that may not be denied. You must beware, however, of an assumption which, irrespective of the words used or linguistic conventions, is merely tautologous.

5.3
FINDING THE SOLUTION

TH EN ADD . . . .

Having located those passages containing the judge's reasoning you may now reflect of what he has achieved:

- Did the judge solve the major problem he was addressing in the course of his judgment?

- In the course of doing so did he raise new ones?

- Did he acknowledge problems he could not solve?

An interpretative reading is concerned with finding out what the judge's solutions are, and how he has argued those solutions. It is by argument that a court acquaints itself sufficiently intimately and accurately with the material facts of the case; from such facts will emerge certain possible rules which may be applied to them. The parties contend for either a different interpretation or a different application of such rules to the facts.

The task of the advocate is to establish a certain proposition by a series of logical steps. In order to do so he will press into service any material that may assist the logical process. Nothing can be more conclusive for his purpose than to show that the proposition for which he contends has previously been established in the same or similar circumstances. Thus counsel will rely as much as possible on precedents as being the shortest and clearest way to his objective. But he will seldom find an exact analogy in previous cases. If he is fortunate enough to do so he has disposed of the matter, assuming the analogy is exact, because the logical process is completed at once. But in the very great majority of cases there is no precise authority. He must then find other analogies and turn to arguments from other sources, legal, historical, formal or material, or whatever else it may be which reasonably support his contention and are logically relevant.

Effective legal argument is not confined to binding precedent. It may have recourse to the opinion of reputable writers, decisions of other countries, history, common sense, natural justice, convenience and utility, to the etymology and interpretation of words, to anything that may legitimately come within the ambit of dialectical demonstration. Providing he builds up his thesis consistently the Court will not greatly care whether he culls his arguments from dry propositions of law or the flowers of rhetoric and poetry.[13]

Once the judge has absorbed, considered, determined, adopted and/or rejected counsel's argument, his own reasoning itself comes under scrutiny.

- Did he discriminate between the kind of argument that points to one or more particular facts as evidence for some generalisation (*i.e.* did he apply inductive reasoning) or the kind that offers a series of general statements to prove some further generalisation (deductive reasoning)? For the purpose of close analysis of the units of reasoning it is important to discriminate between those two.

- Did he recognise that logical elements are not all of equal weight? If it is a man's business to adjudicate between rival contentions he will soon develop guiding rules, explicit or implicit, for distinguishing degrees of cogency in the arguments addressed to him, in the same way that if it is a man's business to argue habitually he will soon learn to discriminate between the stronger and the weaker of his materials.[14] If so, was his weighing of the rival contentions correct?

- Was his acceptance or rejection of a proposition based on its proof by reasoning or its establishment by experiment? Sometimes it is possible to support a proposition by both reasoning from other general truths and by offering experimental evidence. Sometimes only one method is available. This may be of particular importance in a case that turns on, or is largely influenced by expert evidence outside the immediate experience of the judge.

- Consider the judge's approach to the proof of a fact or proposition: observe what things the judge says he must *assume*, what he says has been *proved*, and what need not be proved because they are self-evident. He may honestly try to tell you what all his assumptions are or he may just as honestly leave you to find them out for yourself. Not everything can be proved just as not everything can be defined. Such things as axioms and assumptions or postulates are needed for the proof of other propositions. These, if proved, can be used as premises in further proofs.

- Is the logical basis for the judge's argument sound? The role of the advocate is to persuade. Psychologically it is much more effective in arguing a case to dress up sentiment with logic. In delivering judgment there is a tendency on the part of judges to do the same. This is particu-

---

[13] See *Precedent and Logic* C.K.Allen (1925) CLXIII LQR 332.
[14] Ibid 333.

larly so where the judge starts with a conclusion and afterwards tries to find some premise which will substantiate it.

- Is the validity of the argument based on the width of a major premise? There is a real danger when applying syllogistic reasoning to law that an attractive but wide proposition obscures the real question at issue: thus, for example in *Rose* v *Ford* [1937] AC 826 the House of Lords criticises the Court of Appeal for its logic in awarding separate personal injury damages in a fatal accident case:

> "This way of looking at the case involves in my judgment a failure to give effect to s. 1 of the Act of 1934. The moment before the girl died there was, as I think, apart from her actual death a cause of action vested in her for deprivation or loss of expectation of life. Before the Act, that cause of action would have ceased with her death. That same cause of action, by force of the Act, now survives in the administrator. It is not correct to say that the administrator acquires under the Act a new or changed cause of action, as would be the case if he were a third party suing for the deceased's death. Obviously she could not have sued herself for her own death. The administrator simply stands in the shoes of the deceased, and in a sense may be said to continue her life. The damages for loss of expectation of life are indeed on a different footing from those for loss of the leg. The former damages are to be based on her state as a young and healthy woman with the use of both legs at the moment before she was struck down. If in addition she got damages for the loss of her leg for the period of the normal expectation of life, she would be getting pro tanto damages twice over. *But on the view of the Court of Appeal the defendant would be in the paradoxical position of being entitled to plead in mitigation of damage that he had not merely maimed but killed the plaintiff. It was some such idea that before the Act of 1934 inspired the cynical comment that it was cheaper to kill than to maim or cripple.* The Act has, however, not merely stated that it is amending the law as to the effect of death in relation to causes of action, but has done so. The fact that the plaintiff has died before judgment is now in truth an irrelevant circumstance, save that it obviates to some extent the necessity of medical evidence that the accident has shortened the person's life. The damage claimed is not for the death, for which the victim herself could not have sued, any more than the administrator can who merely stands in her shoes. I venture respectfully to think that the view of the Court of Appeal illustrates a tendency common in construing an Act which changes the law, that is, to minimize or neutralize its operation by introducing notions taken from or inspired by the

old law which the words of the Act were intended to abrogate and
did abrogate.

*A similar tendency is illustrated, I think, by the references to a dogma of
somewhat obscure import and uncertain application, that in a civil court the
death of a human being cannot be complained of as an injury...*"[15]

Or consider the logic of Simonds J in determining whether the sale of cigarettes in a tea shop in 1940 rendered the tenant in breach of the terms of its
lease:

"In these circumstances the question which I have to determine is
this. First, does the ABC shop carry on, on these premises, the business
of the sale of tobacco, cigars and cigarettes? Secondly, if such a
business is carried on on these premises, have the defendants
permitted or suffered the premises to be used so that they are liable on
their covenant with the plaintiffs?

I think that I may fairly say, as was said in a somewhat similar case,
that this is a very puzzling point. Ultimately, I think that it is to be
solved by asking oneself whether, on the fair meaning of the covenant
and according to the ordinary use of language, it can be predicated of
the ABC tea-shop that there is there carried on the business of the sale
of tobacco, cigars and cigarettes. It is, I think, at least clear that it
cannot be predicated of the ABC that they carry on on these premises
the business of tobacconists. Nobody, on being asked the question
whether they carry on there the business of tobacconists, would
answer that question in the affirmative.

I ask next whether there is any difference for this purpose between
carrying on the business of a tobacconist and carrying on the business
of the sale of tobacco, cigars and cigarettes. One must give a meaning,
if possible, to every part of an instrument carefully drawn and entered
into between the parties. Since the words "business of a tobacconist"
and "business of the sale of tobacco, cigars and cigarettes" occur in
immediate proximity in the same clause, I must assume that some
difference was intended between the two phrases. I am disposed to
think that here there is some difference between the two and that,
even though the business of tobacconist as a whole was not carried
on, yet the provision would be infringed if it could fairly be said that
the business of the sale of tobacco, cigars and cigarettes was carried
on. I have therefore to consider that question.

---

[15] Per Lord Wright @ 845.

I find it difficult to take the view that anybody being asked this question: "What is the business which the ABC carry on at this shop?" would reply: "They carry on several businesses; they carry on the business of selling refreshments; they carry on the business of selling confectionery; they carry on the business of selling tobacco, cigars and cigarettes."

In my view, what is done at these premises is the carrying on of the business of a tea-shop, and that involves, among other things, the sale of cigarettes. It is common – indeed, I was told that it was almost universal – that in tea-shops of this character cigarettes should be sold. Accordingly, it appears to me that it is no more right to predicate of this shop that there is carried on there the business of the sale of tobacco, cigars and cigarettes than to say of it that there is carried on the business of the sale of milk, or the business of the sale of confectionery. There is there carried on the usual business of a tea-shop, which involves the sale of a number of articles therein usually sold."

- Did the judge consider the impact and wider effect of his judgment and use the process to reality test?

5.4

THE DOMESTIC APPROACH

Sir John Salmond wrote[16] that the English judge is not merely a mechanic who broadcasts rules of law to the community. To administer law is to administer justice and justice is wider than law, containing those principles of natural justice, practical expediency, or common sense and so supplement existing law. On the whole the method of common law judicial reasoning combines a conscientious search for true justice with the logical application of legal conceptions to actual circumstances. It is open to persuasive influences which have a good claim to respect and consideration.

Judges of an English common law background are readily able to determine questions concerning the existence of a rule, or the choice between two competing rules, or the validity of a rule, as questions of law, and the credibility of a witness or inference to be drawn from evidence as matters of fact. Likewise their approach to evidential and procedural questions, and the grant or refusal of remedies in the exercise of a discretion is based on experience drawn from practice.

Since the principal task of the judge is to adjudicate upon disputes that have already occurred, with his attention being fixed on the past, a judge's methodology in dealing with a variety of cases may be inconsistent, but it is ascertainable. This is true not only in relation to his approach to the facts, but also in relation to the standards which it is appropriate for him to apply to the dispute. Just as it would be wrong for the judge to apply to the dispute the superseded standards of a past age, so it would be incorrect to apply standards merely because they might seem appropriate to circumstances likely to exist in the future. In general justice requires that the solution to a dispute be forged from such considerations as could and should have guided the parties conduct when the dispute arose.

---

[16] *Jurisprudence* Salmond 7th edn. (P&MI) 187 note 2.

Analysis is more difficult when judgments are collegial, as in the experience of European courts in particular, where there is no provision for dissenting judgments, a stylised format, and the prose used, even allowing for the vagaries of translating professional jargon, is stylistically flat. Joint decisions may reflect something of a compromise by tribunal members who would like to offer at least some dissent, but see no useful purpose in doing so. But of greater concern is the fact that collegial judgments have a tendency to lack the detailed factual and legal analysis of English courts in favour of very logical development where a point follows each point in the order of logical sequence. Other commentators have suggested[17] that this is advantageous and an approach which domestic tribunals would be better to develop as these judgments are easier to read and understand.

What you need to unearth, either properly to understand the judge's thinking, or to challenge him intellectually, are those points of uncertainty or argument that do not fit into the rational deductive process. Unlike their counterparts in Europe, common law judges are not reluctant to explore the implications of their judgments or their impact on the boundaries of the law beyond issues directly raised by case in hand, even if they shy away from making policy indications on questions lacking general importance. Frequently our judges speculate on the scope and implications of their judgment as a valuable part of the process of reasoning. It is here that the most valuable material is likely to be available to the analytical reader.

---

[17] *Learning Legal Rules* J.A.Holland & J.S.Webb 5th edn. OUP 2003 p.83.

5.5

JUDICIAL REASONING AND THE ROLE OF PERSUASION

In reading any judgment you must consider: what is the judge's objective, and what means for achieving this is he proposing? His objective is to persuade you that his decision is justified; the method he uses is advocacy, just as much as those who appear before him. His argument appeals to the mind, to reason, to the senses and to emotion, to gain direction of your will. Ultimately the effect of the judgment will turn on whether or not you accept his argument.

In the nature of practical things men have to be persuaded to think and act in a certain way.[18] The person who reads intelligently and knows basic terms, propositions and arguments, will always be able to detect oratory and to spot passages that make an emotive or overelaborate use of words. You yourself will look for reasoning, and assess whether it is either good or not, in relation to the material facts.

For the purpose of fair criticism we need to consider, in broad terms, the questions, what does the judge want to prove? Whom does he want to convince? What special knowledge does he assume? What special language does he use? Does he really know what he is talking about – enough to give a fair and balanced view of the situation? We recognise that a judge cannot suppose, guess, hypothecate or estimate except under very carefully controlled circumstances. We are therefore entitled to investigate his assumptions, starting from the position that there may always be a doubt whether they are reasonable or not, particularly in circumstances where historical facts prove elusive; or where there has been a condensation of the detailed evidence or information provided in the judgment, such that it is possible to argue what has been left out becomes critical.

---

[18] See *Adler op. cit.* p.198.

5.6

DISTINGUISHING GRAMMATICAL AND LOGICAL INTERPRETATION

You must distinguish between your grammatical or linguistic analysis of a judgment, and your interpretation of the judge's logic and reasoning. To do this:

- First divide up the judgment into convenient units and assess their contents;

- See how the arguments are worked up in logical progressions or towers, as propositions become grouped together as terms;

- Identify whether assumptions are supported by reasons;

- By contrast, note separately the use of specific legal language:

Sentences and paragraphs are grammatical units and units of language. Propositions and arguments are logical units or units of thought and knowledge.[19] Because language is not a perfect medium for the expression of thought, particularly the use of legal language where one word may have many meanings and two or more words can have the same meaning, or at least closely similar meanings, the relationship between a judge's vocabulary and his terminology is complicated. One word may represent several terms, such as 'immunity', and one term may be represented by several words, for example 'fair, just and reasonable'. The difficulty with language becomes important when one remembers that to data search a judgment or report it is the language that is applied in the search, not legal concepts.

---

[19] *Ibid* p. 117.

5.7
POSITIVE JUDICIAL ARGUMENT

Judgments are opinions based on reasoned propositions. A proposition is an expression of the judge's judgment about something: he either affirms something he thinks is true or denies something he judges to be false. A proposition of this sort is a declaration of knowledge, not intention. Therefore you should not be satisfied with knowing what the judge's opinions are. His propositions are nothing but expressions of personal opinion unless they are supported by reasons. You should want to know not merely what his propositions are but why he thinks you should be persuaded to accept them.

Adler suggests[20] that an argument is always a set or series of statements of which some provide the grounds or reasons for what is to be concluded. A common example contained in judgments is the use of related statements: *this* is said *because* of *that*; if *this* is so then *that* must follow; or, since *this* therefore *that*; it follows from this, that that is the case.

A paragraph or at least a collection of sentences is required to express an argument. The premises or principles of an argument may not always be stated first, but they are the source of the conclusion, nevertheless. If the argument is valid, the conclusion follows from the premises. For these purposes you must consider each of the premises, since even if you accept that a conclusion must flow from two or more premises, you must consider whether one or all of the premises that support it may be false.

---

[20] *Ibid* p.115.

5.8
AIDS TO REASONING

Despite strong media assertions that members of the judiciary live in ivory towers, most judges share the common experiences of the litigants they are called upon to judge: they read newspapers and watch television; they use public transport; they share the experiences of being spouses, parents and grandparents; they are consumers like everyone else; they have health problems like everyone else; and they indulge in social recreation, including popular recreation. In his reasoning a judge will apply what he regards as common sense and his daily observation of the world in which we live.

Common experiences do not have to be shared by everyone in order to be common. *Common* is not the same thing as *universal*. One does not need the extrinsic aid of special experiences in order to understand them. But such experiences, whether common or special, give rise to a recognised standard, whether of behaviour or performance, to which a judge is properly entitled to have regard.

The application of what is called common sense, being a presumed rational and general if unexpressed understanding about a matter, has long been recognised as an aid to judicial reasoning. Often, with the benefit of hindsight, practitioners will regard a decision as a matter of common sense; equally on occasion they will protest that by a particular decision the law offends against common sense.

The question of special experience is mainly relevant to the use of expert opinion, often in the reading of scientific or technical works. Judges require such special experience in order to come to a proper understanding of scientific or technical expert reports, the basis for the arguments they contain, and at its most basic level, to be able to follow scientific or other expert evidence.

5.9

THE JUDGE AND THE EXPERT

Judges are called upon daily to determine disputes whose subjects may be scientific, technological or highly specialised so far as a particular trade, profession or industry is concerned. These may require an explanation of some or all of the material trade or technical jargon, methodology, professional standards, custom and practice, and both national and internationally recognised norms and models. Often the issue centres upon what is the relevant professional standard or trade practice, and whether liability occurs because a defendant has departed from such a standard or usage.

Where such matters are outside the experience or knowledge of the court, evidence of expert opinion in connection with the material issues will be called on if it will assist the judge in his decision-making process. There are three fundamentals of which we occasionally lose sight:

- The expert is *not* the judge, and does not perform his function;

- Although based on recognised qualification and experience, ultimately expert evidence is only opinion;

- Like any other evidence that is received, the judge is free to reject it.

The judge should not be in awe of an expert, and should try and treat such evidence with as much measured detachment as he would any other. Making allowances for the inherent respect due to expertise, experience and authority, the judge should nonetheless deal with weight and materiality with great care. In assessing the regard he has had to an expert when delivering judgment, you will wish to analyse whether the judge has ascertained:

- The relevance of the expert's qualifications to the facts in issue;

- The relevance of the expert's experience to the facts in issue;[21]

---

[21] *National Justice Compania Naviera SA* v *Prudential Assurance Co Ltd* ('*The Ikarian Reefer*') [1995] 1 Lloyd's Rep 455 CA per Stuart-Smith LJ @ 496.497.

- Whether the evidence has been given with true impartiality and lack of partisanship. If there is a dispute between experts of similar relevant standing, is it a 'genuine' or 'partisan' conflict?

- Whether the evidence has been of primary assistance to the court, or whether it is being used to corroborate evidence of fact or assertions of method;

- The true weight that should properly be attached to it.

Essentially the judge should have asked the questions:

- Is the expert neutral?

- Is the expert reliable?

- Is the expert representative?

- Is the expert's evidence relevant and material?

The area in which judges meet most criticism concerning experts is in case management. Part 35 of the Civil Procedure Rules 1998 was intended to reduce the number of experts and have those appointed come to a consensus. It was also designed to reduce the risk of bias by requiring experts to certify their understanding of their overriding duty to the court. In assessing the outcome of any case involving experts you will wish to examine how the judge's case management impacted on expert evidence, particularly in terms of the four criteria referred to above, and even more so when evidence of expert opinion was taken from a single joint appointee. Certainly the conduct of experts can now be the subject of almost as much examination as the substance of what they have said.[22]

For ease of reference judges like experts to provide them with a norm or constant against which they can measure the conduct of the defendant. This enables them to both rationalise and simplify their decision making. However, although produced for the assistance of the court, expert evidence is not always designed or shaped for the contingencies of litigation, particularly in areas of science, technology and medicine. Here, and in other areas where new developments and continuing research may challenge existing benchmarks of expert opinion, the idea of a normal standard tends to be idealised by the courts. There is a presumption that research results are open and accessible, and that scientific or technical knowledge is shared communally with all working for the common good, and thus that each expert has access to the same material.

---

[22] See for example *Selman* v *Vijay Construction (UK) Ltd* [2003] EWHC TCC 1100 HH Judge Thornton QC unrep. 8 May 2003.

This is a somewhat naïve approach. Experts may be in competition with each other, particularly in a narrow field. They will wish to protect research work. They may have personal, cultural, financial or professional reasons for attaining primacy through presenting or publishing an opinion based on incomplete, partial or under-theorised results. This may be unknown to the client as well as the courts.

The judge has to determine whether the witness is providing evidence of expert opinion which is representative of the norm, or whether his evidence is novel and maverick, or in some other way only recognised by a small minority in the relevant scientific or technical community. The evidence may have been taken out of context; it may have been drawn from abstract statements, or statements only relevant where certain background assumptions, facts and interpretations are vital. As 'novel' evidence it may not altogether be accepted by the wider scientific community, or, at a slightly lower level, there may not exist anything approximating to universal support among, for example, scientists for a particular interpretation.

There has to be general acceptance of a scientific or medical principle for it to be admitted into evidence in the United States. In Australia[23] and England[24] courts have been willing to admit evidence purportedly accepted by a minority in a particular field, if it comes within the compass of a 'recognised body of opinion'.

The judge, then, has to fall back on the analytical and reasoning skills he applies to other categories of evidence, namely assessing materiality, reliability and weight, in viewing the expert. He may wish to consider such matters as:

- Are the norms used by the experts consistent or inconsistent with each other or with any other published measured standards?

- What is the degree of certainty being espoused?

- Whether any boundaries been crossed between different professional activities?

- The impression given by the demeanour and authority of the expert?

- Whether the expert is being dogmatic or flexible in his opinion?

- Notwithstanding that the expert has all relevant professional information, has he taken in the facts of the case adequately?

---

[23] *R v Gilmore* [1977] 2 NSWLR 935 @939–941; *Runjanjic and Kontinen v The Queen* (1991) 56 SASR 114, 119; *R v Rose* (1993) A Crim R 1, 9; *R v J* (1994) 75 A Crim R 522, 535–6; *R v Jarrett* (1994) 62 SASR 443.
[24] *Maynard v West Midlands Regional Health Authority* [1984] 1 WLR 634 @ 639; *Bolitho v City and Hackney Health Authority* [1998] AC 232, 238–239, 241–242.

You will recognise that judges are faced with entirely novel evidence as science and technology makes advances. A good example is the use of DNA as receivable evidence in criminal cases. The use of a specific advance in technology had to be considered by the courts: once a number of decisions have been made concerning the use of specific technology it becomes easier for subsequent courts to base their decisions on earlier authority. Each subsequent decision tends to reinforce the development of a judicial consensus. This can refer to a body of knowledge rather than a separate single advance in medicine or computer science or an industrial process.

Finally one of the judge's basic tasks is to choose between experts of differing opinion. He must be able to show that has a reasoned basis for his preference: the factors by which he has drawn a distinction may be categorised as:

(i)   What the witnesses have actually said;
(ii) The extent to which what they have said is lent authority by their respective qualifications and experience;
(iii) The relationship between their respective qualification and experience and the task in hand;
(iv) Where the weight of the evidence in terms of general principle lies, i.e. the novelty of the propositions being advanced, and the relative support of the technical or scientific community to which the expert is attached to their norm or model.

5.10

THE USE OF PRECEDENT

"A case is only an authority for what it actually decides. I entirely deny that it can be quoted for a proposition that may seem to flow logically from it. Such a mode or reasoning assumes that the law is necessarily a logical code, whereas every lawyer must acknowledge that the law is not always logical at all."[25]

"Judging is a practical matter, and an act of will. Notwithstanding all the apparatus of authority, the judge nearly always has some degree of choice"[26]

The use of a system of binding precedent is more recent than you would think. The hierarchy of authority did not finally establish itself until comparatively late in the nineteenth century. This appears not to have been by the result of any single direction or framework imposed by the higher courts, but as the natural consequence of the enormous growth of printed decisions and regularisation of semi-official laws reports in 1865. In our own era the scope and range of law reports have undergone a huge expansion over the last 20 years, even before the development of electronic reports, the use of daily alerters and media-neutral citation. In order to prevent being swamped with authority the courts now try to cap the list of citations produced by counsel.[27] What will result from the ongoing further expansion of available authority remains to be seen.

The debate over the rigidity of a system of binding authority went on throughout the twentieth century, much of it being concerned with whether judge-made law was a good thing.[28] In 1925 Carleton Kemp Allen wrote.[29] "the

---

[25] Lord Halsbury LC *Quinn v Leathem [1901] AC 506.*
[26] *Legal Essays and Addresses* Lord Wright 1939 p 25.
[27] *Practice Direction (Judgments: Form and Citation)* [2001] 1 WLR 194 para 2.5; *Practice Direction (Court of Appeal: Citation of Authorities)* [2001] 1 WLR 1001; CPR Part 52 PD (30th June 2004) para 15.11(2)(a); and see *Scribes West Ltd v Relsa Anstalt (No 1) [2004] EWCA (Civ) 835* per Brooke LJ.
[28] "There is in fact no such thing as judge-made law, though they frequently have to apply existing law to circumstances as to which it has not previously been authoritatively laid down that such law is applicable" *Williams v Baddeley [1892] 2 QB 324* per Lord Esher MR @ 326.
[29] *Precedent and Logic* C.K.Allen 1925 CLXIII LQR 329.

conspicuous advantage of a system of precedents is that legal principles are framed, not merely as conceptions *in abstracto*, but as practical rules operating *in concreto*. Granted that a judgment is the construction of a legal proposition, and not a mechanical application of sovereign commandments already formulated, there can be no better foundation for the process than the collation and analysis of previous workings of the rule in actual cases. Not only is the law kept elastic by the greater scope left to the trained faculties of the judges...we come as near to that uniformity of law which is said to be more desirable than ideal but uncertain justice...Judgments give rise to binding standards... It is an open secret that judges have a good deal of choice in the way in which they apply case law and they are prone to distinguish even the most closely similar precedent if they feel strongly that it tends towards an undesirable result."

5.11

PRECEDENT AND REASONING

The system of precedent is the foundation of legal reasoning in the common law: a proposition of law is established; a similarity is identified in a following case, and the proposition is then applied to the degree or level of generality which may embrace the facts in question in the preceding decision. The judge is therefore reasoning by example, a mechanism by which his finding of fact is applied to a specific legal consequence. Since this application may or may not be appropriate in the different factual situation of a later case, a different result may be yielded. It is the level of generality or particularity of the proposition combined with the facts of the case that determines whether the legal rule contained in the precedent applies.

The judicial process is engaged in selecting the appropriate law and applying it to the facts as found. On the facts and arguments before him the judge arrives at certain conclusions. These he develops into a judgment by building up, piece by piece, a structure of logic in which he may use any material that he considers appropriate, is supportive of his conclusion and, if necessary (but *only* if necessary), moves the law in the direction of the remedy he intends to provide. He has a plethora of authority to select: these days inventive counsel will cite statutes and delegated legislation, both domestic and European, the most recent comprehensive range of cases from all jurisdictions, ancient and modern texts, Hansard, Law Commission reports, parliamentary papers, learned articles and the thinking of eminent foreign jurists.

Fortunately the judge follows certain well-established rules in selecting materials of different relative values. His whole training, drawn from practice as well as the bench, instructs him that the most conclusive logic is the analogy of antecedent cases, especially if courts of a higher jurisdiction than his own have decided them. Since these bind him, the direction in which he must travel is laid out before him. But, as has been said,[30] he is only bound intellectually by the established logic which it his profession to exercise, not in any automatic or mechanical manner. In reality he can flout precedent. No principle in the textbooks can make him a machine. It is he himself who must

---

[30] *Ibid* p. 333.

decide whether the precedent is authoritative or not. The most Olympian decision of the House of Lords will not bind a county court judge unless he thinks he ought to be bound by it – unless he thinks it presents a clear and relevant analogy to the case before him – and on that point opinions may greatly differ. Allen[31] puts it this way:

> "The binding force of precedents has, through constant and often unthinking repetition, become a kind of sacramental phrase which contains a large element of fiction. If a court is quite clear about the rule of law which should be applied to the case before it, it will seldom allow itself to be embarrassed by an inconvenient decision. There are many ways of 'distinguishing,' and a bad case which runs counter to the *communis opinion doctorum* is soon distinguished out of existence. When, in 1923, the House of Lords definitely overruled *Miller v Hancock* [1893] 2 QB 177 in *Fairman v Perpetual Investment Co* [1923] AC 74 it merely gave the earlier decision its *coup de grace*; it had been on the point of death for twenty years, because single judges, as well as the Court of Appeal, had repeatedly 'distinguished' it in ways which were more ingenious than ingenuous. What judge, save a pedant, would consider himself bound by *Gibbons v Proctor* (1892) 64 LT 594? It is simply pronounced 'bad law' and if all else fails, the blame for its badness can be laid at the door of the reporter."

And Lord Hobhouse said in *R v Governor of Brockhill Prison, Ex p. Evans (No 2):*[32]

> "any legal decision is no more than evidence of the law. In the *Lincoln City Council* case [1999] 2 AC 349, 377, Lord Goff of Chieveley quoted from *Hale's Common Law of England*, 6th ed (1820), p 90 and *Blackstone's Commentaries*, 6th ed (1774), pp 88–89:
>
>> "the decisions of the courts do not constitute the law properly so called, but are evidence of the law and as such 'have a great weight and authority in expounding, declaring, and publishing what the law of this Kingdom is'."
>
> They are a source of law but not a conclusive source. Judicial decisions are only conclusive as between the parties to them and their privies. The doctrine of precedent may give certain decisions a more authoritative status but this is relative as the present case shows: the Divisional Court was at liberty not to follow its own previous decision. A decision or judgment may on examination be shown to be inconsistent with other decisions. The value,

---

[31] *Ibid* p. 334.
[32] [2001] 2 AC 19 HL @ 45.

force and effect of any decision is a matter to be considered and assessed. They are not statutes which (subject to European Union law) have an absolute and incontrovertible status.

Modern examples of the processes described by Allen abound: either the gradual chipping away of an accepted approach because it no longer reflects contemporary social attitudes, or a subsequent *mores* thinks that it was wrongly decided;[33] or the higher courts require a change in the ebb and flow of a wider principle of law over the course of time either for practical purposes or reasons of policy.[34]

This is not to suggest that precedent is anything other than of the highest importance to our system. It is the most powerful instrument in the logical process; but it is only one, if the chief among many. What judges look for is not some kind of 'revealed' authority that will miraculously settle the problem before them, but a convincing statement or application of a principle of law appropriate to the case in hand.[35] Clearly you will come across what appears to be a number of difficulties regularly thrown up by any rigid system of authority: first, there is the dilemma between two conflicting decisions of courts of superior jurisdiction which may appear to be completely irreconcilable until the issue is decided from above.[36] Second, and perhaps more often, a judge is sometimes bound by precedent to give a decision contrary to his own conviction, very often hoping it will be reversed on appeal. He often hints as much in a first instance judgment, or else distinguishes on the basis that the prior court felt bound by a decision subsequently overruled.[37] When this happens it is unsatisfactory to both the parties and the judge. Third, by the time it reaches the ultimate tribunal, judicial opinion on a point may be almost equally divided, counting all the judges in all the courts concerned.[38] This surely dilutes the value of the decision.

Any common lawyer will be familiar with a multitude of rules for which particular precedents can be cited as authority, particularly where the rule itself derives from the name of the case by which it was established e.g. *Rylands v Fletcher*[39] or *Foakes v Beer*.[40] In most scenarios there will be little doubt about its meaning and operation, particularly where the judge beginning or developing the precedent has spelt out with care the rule and it may have been

---

[33] See for example *R. v R.* (*op.cit.*).
[34] See for example *Arthur J. Hall v Simons* (*op.cit.*).
[35] *Precedent and Logic* C.K.Allen *op.cit.* p. 334.
[36] See for example *Di Palma v Victoria Square Property Co Ltd* [1986] Ch 150 CA overruling *Jones v Barnett* [1984] Ch 500.
[37] See *Haste v Sandell Perkins Ltd* [1984] QB 735 per Hirst J @ 738.
[38] See for example *Arthur J. Hall v Simons* (op.cit.).
[39] [1868] LR 3 HL 330.
[40] (1884) 9 App. Cas. 605, itself a case where the House of Lords reaffirmed a rule which it did not like solely out of respect for precedent.

accepted authoritatively in subsequent cases. There really need to be unusual features that are sufficient to enable the present case to fall outside the ambit of such an existing rule, otherwise a judge has no choice but to apply it. The decision itself then becomes another precedent for the rule and entrenches it further. Frequent judicial endorsement of a rule supported by precedent does give it a special status.

On the other hand judges that afterwards distinguish the precedent will later qualify the original proposition or may even rationalize it on an altogether different basis. In the end nothing may be left of the legal rule which the judge envisaged but a proposition which embodies only all the factual elements of the case which he decided. Judges almost invite a reappraisal of their judgment when formulating a proposed *ratio decidendi* in very general terms, i.e. which may bring within its focus a wide range of disparate cases. A rule of thumb is the more superior the court, the wider can be the ratio. This represents that part of the function of the higher courts which is to give practical guidance to judges at first instance. Good examples may be found historically in the law of privity of contract,[41] and much more recently on causation,[42] and proximity[43] in the recoverability of damage.

---

[41] *Dunlop Pneumatic Tyre Co* v *Selfridge* [1915] AC 847 HL.
[42] *South Australian Asset Management Co. Ltd.* v *York Montague* (op.cit.).
[43] *Sutradhar* v *National Environmental Research Council* [2004] EWCA Civ 175; [2004] PNLR 30.

5.12

AT THE COAL FACE: TRIAL JUDGES

Judges working at a lower level are concerned principally with the facts before them, and to engage in the adjudicative process as efficiently and, perhaps, conveniently as possible. By and large first instance judges do not like to make new law. They tend to work intuitively, within general legal concepts and look for precedent only where the facts of a relevant authority and facts of the case before the court are either indistinguishable or substantially the same. Judges at first instance are most happy when the finding of facts alone determines the outcome of a case, and will avoid becoming enmeshed in legal argument unnecessarily if they can. If a trial judge has to consider legal issues he usually first finds the facts, then looks at the relevance of a previous case and decides whether the legal reasoning in the previous case be compared and applied to facts before him. He will not wish to make new law, far less give vent to any policy considerations. Even the higher courts tend to shy away from making policy indications on questions lacking general importance, and to the surprise of many advocates appearing before it, the House of Lords is as equally concerned with the factual matrix of a case as the puisne judge.

Judges, like any other professionals, require both confidence and experience to arrive at firm conclusions. Even the most experienced judge may be troubled by an oddity or perhaps the general peculiarity of a situation with which he is faced. He may be dissatisfied with submissions by the advocates appearing on both sides. He may be troubled by a recent authority that appears to be out of step with his own thinking or a common sense approach to solving the problem. Or he may face real uncertainty as to what to do.

While there is no formal mentoring process, judges, and particularly deputies and Recorders, are encouraged to seek advice when they need it, and if necessary, to adjourn cases briefly in order to do so. It may be that they can seek the advice of senior colleagues in the mess over lunch, if a large court centre, or to call upon a judge with more specialist knowledge.

Judges in the lower courts also tend to be conscious of the disapproval in the profession of intellectual dishonesty. "Distinguishing" is sometimes an ingenious intellectual contrivance to avoid having to follow an inconvenient previous decision which would otherwise bind the court. There are many examples worthy of study.[44]

As a member of the community the judge is bound to share more or less its common thinking and accepted wisdom, and indeed judges often express sympathy with such notions when they find themselves reluctantly constrained by an earlier precedent to decide a case in conflict with what must seem reasonable to the layman. It may be that a case such as *Howard* v *Walker*[45] where Lord Goddard CJ was obliged to say:[46]

> "It may be that the law is not entirely satisfactory on this point. No doubt, it is difficult for a layman to understand why, if he is walking along a road and slips into an excavation at the side of it, he should be entitled to recover, whereas if he slips into the excavation as he is endeavouring to get on to the road, he is not, but I must take the law as I find it."

would today be decided differently for precisely the reason that a layman would otherwise find the law unintelligible or lacking in common sense.

The development of the common law is essentially a sophisticated process of refinement in which a later and usually superior court examines previous authority to decide whether the *ratio* of the present case falls within or outside its scope. It evolves by identifying material differences, great or small, and determining whether the rule or proposition in question applies to these, and if so why and to what effect. The application affects not only the decision in hand but also the prior case, since the process of the superior court is to affirm, apply, approve, consider, distinguish, overrule, or reverse the previous decision.

---

[44] *Taylor* v *Webb* [1937] 2 KB 283; *Rothwell* v *Caverswall Stone* [1944] 2 All ER 350; *Fisher* v *Ruislip-Northwood UDC* [1945] KB 584; *Brown* v *Davies* [1958] 1 QB 117; *D* v *East Berkshire CH NHS Trust* [2003] 4 All ER 796.

[45] [1947] 2 All ER 197.

[46] @ p.199.

5.13
DISTINGUISHING YOUR JUDGMENT

It becomes essential in your analysis to have a scheme or checklist of items that will assist you in assessing whether the judge can properly distinguish authority which would otherwise bind him.

- Identify whether the issue is really a proposition of law or a question of fact (called by an older generation a proposition of good sense). In *Qualcast (Wolverhampton) Ltd* v *Haynes* [1959] AC 743 HL both Lord Somervell and Lord Denning drew attention to the distinction:

> "A judge naturally gives reasons for the conclusion formerly arrived at by a jury without reasons. It may sometimes be difficult to draw the line, but if the reasons given by a judge for arriving at the conclusion previously reached by a jury are to be treated as "law" and citable, the precedent system will die from a surfeit of authorities. In *Woods* v *Durable Suites Ltd.* [1953] 1 W.L.R. 857; [1953] 2 All E.R. 391. counsel for the plaintiff was seeking to rely on a previous decision in a negligence action. Singleton L.J. said this [1953] 1 W.L.R. 857, 860.: "That was a case of the same nature as that which is now under appeal. It is of the greatest importance that it should be borne in mind that though the nature of the illness and the nature of the work are the same, the facts were quite different. Mr. Doughty claims that the decision of this court in *Clifford* v *Charles H. Challen & Son Ltd.* [1951] 1 K.B. 495; [1951] 1 T.L.R. 234; [1951] 1 All E.R. 72. lays down a standard to be adopted in a case of this nature. In other words, he seeks to treat that decision as deciding a question of law rather than as being a decision on the facts of that particular case."

> In the present case, and I am not criticising him, the learned county court judge felt himself bound by certain observations in different cases which were not, I think, probably intended by the learned judges to enunciate any new principles or gloss on the

familiar standard of reasonable care. It must be a question on the evidence in each case whether, assuming a duty to provide some safety equipment, there is a duty to advise everyone, whether experienced or inexperienced, as to its use."[47]

'My Lords, in 1944 du Parcq L.J. gave a warning which is worth repeating today: "There is danger, particularly in these days when few cases are tried with juries, of exalting to the status of propositions of law what really are particular applications to special facts of propositions of ordinary good sense"; see *Easson* v *London & North Eastern Railway Co.*

In the present case the only proposition of law that was relevant was the well-known proposition – with its threefold sub-division – that it is the duty of a master to take reasonable care for the safety of his workmen. No question arose on that proposition. The question that did arise was this: What did reasonable care demand of the employers in this particular case? That is not a question of law at all but a question of fact. To solve it the tribunal of fact be it judge or jury – can take into account any proposition of good sense that is relevant in the circumstances, but it must beware not to treat it as a proposition of law. I may perhaps draw an analogy from the Highway Code. It contains many propositions of good sense which may be taken into account in considering whether reasonable care has been taken, but it would be a mistake to elevate them into propositions of law.'[48]

- Be aware that a court is more likely to follow precedent than depart from it, since public policy requires consistency: "The need for legal certainty demands that they should be very reluctant to depart from recent fully reasoned decisions unless there are strong grounds to do so." per Lord Slynn in *Lewis* v *Attorney General of Jamaica.*[49]

- Bear in mind that the law is tidal, in the sense that it has an ebb and flow, and particular cases follow a pattern. This is best illustrated where a superior court considers two conflicting lines of authority, for example *Henderson* v *Merrett Syndicates Ltd.*[50] Does the judge's action amount to a radical departure from an established principle?

---

[47] Per Lord Somervell @ 758.
[48] Per Lord Denning @ 759.
[49] [2001] AC 50.
[50] [1995] 2 AC 145.

- Conversely, is the judge building a logical extension from an established principle? There is a positive desire to do justice in the case in hand, and therefore to set a new precedent if that is what the court believes justice requires: see *White* v *Jones*.[51]

- The Court will rarely overturn a long-established legal concept, although it does happen: see *R* v *R* [52]

- Is the present case on all fours with the precedent: what is the extent of similarity or dissimilarity of the material facts?

- Do both cases illustrate the same principle?

- Is the authority distinguishable because one or more material facts contained in the authority are missing from the present case?

- Is the authority distinguishable because one or more material facts in the present case were not present in the earlier case?

- Is the authority distinguishable because the law has moved on? This is of importance in comparing cases before and after the introduction of the Civil Procedure Rules 1998, particularly in procedural matters,[53] and before and after the coming into force of the Human Rights Act 1998 in remedies.

- Is the authority distinguishable as being no longer 'good law' because society has moved on? The argument is founded on a contention that the relevant social and legal environment prevailing at the time of the precedent has changed: see, for example *D. & C. Builders* v *Rees* [1966] 2 QB 617 per Dankwerts LJ @ 626:

  > "the giving of a cheque of the debtor for a smaller amount than the sum due is very different from "the gift of a horse, hawk, or robe, etc." mentioned in *Pinnel's Case*. I accept that the cheque of some other person than the debtor, in appropriate circumstances, may be the basis of an accord and satisfaction, but I cannot see how in the year 1965 the debtor's own cheque for a smaller sum can be better than payment of the whole amount of the debt in cash. The cheque is only conditional payment, it may be difficult to cash, or it may be returned by the bank with the letters "R.D." upon it, unpaid. I think that *Goddard* v. *O'Brien*, either was wrongly decided or should not be followed in the circumstances of today."

---

[51] [1995] 2 AC 207 per Sir Donald Nicholls V-C @ 223H (CA) and per Lord Goff @ 259G. (HL)
[52] [1992] 1 AC 599 @ 614 per Lord Keith *op.cit.*
[53] See *Biguzzi* v *Rank Leisure* [1999] 1 WLR 1926.

A precedent will not be regarded as wrong, but nevertheless may not be followed, where it can be distinguished because societal factual circumstances have changed since it was originally decided: see per Lord Hoffmann in *Lewis v Attorney General of Jamaica*.[54] Similarly a precedent, though correctly decided, may not be followed where related legal principles have changed since the precedent was determined.

- Can the authority be said properly to have been decided *per incuriam* for failing itself to take into account prior relevant cases? A precedent may not be followed if it is found to be *per incuriam*, that is where relevant statutory provisions or binding case law authority have been overlooked or misinterpreted in arriving at the holding in the precedent: see Lord Hoffman in *Lewis*.[55]

- Can the authority be conveniently avoided as being 'persuasive' only, and having no true binding force?

- Can the authority be said to have been simply wrongly decided? In *R v Kansal (No.2)*[56] a majority of the members of the Appellate Committee held that a precedent may be held to be wrong and justify overruling where it is found from a practical point of view to be unworkable. Lord Hoffmann in *Lewis*[57] went so far as to say that a case could be not followed as it was 'merely wrong' i.e. wrongly reasoned or came to a wrong conclusion.

- Can the authority be said to have placed too great an emphasis on fact 'a' when the present case requires an emphasis on facts 'b' and 'c'?

- Can the authority be shown to have an inconclusive *ratio* or *rationes*? This concerns the type of judicial spree for which Lord Denning became famous, the presentation of independent lines of reasoning not touched upon by arguments, the hallmark of impatient judges trying to set the law to right. Such an approach was the subject of explicit disapproval in *Rahimtoola v Nizam of Hyderabad*[58] where Lord Denning was criticized by Vicount Simonds.[59] Lord Reid[60] and Viscount Somervell.[61]

> "My Lords, I must add that, since writing this opinion, I have had the privilege of reading the opinion which my noble and learned friend, Lord Denning, is about to deliver. It is right that I should say that I must not be taken as assenting to his views upon a

---

[54] *op.cit.* @ p. 90.
[55] *Ibid.*
[56] [2001] UKHL 62; [2001] 3 WLR 1562.
[57] *Op.cit.* @ p.89.
[58] [1958] AC 379 HL.
[59] *Ibid* @ 398.
[60] *Ibid* @ 404.
[61] *Ibid* @ 410.

> number of questions and authorities in regard to which the
> House has not had the benefit of the arguments of counsel or of
> the judgment of the courts below."

- Is the authority based on an absence of argument? It is well settled that a
  proposition of law which passes *sub silentio*, i.e. neither supported nor
  contested in argument by counsel but assumed to be correct without
  mention by the court, is not binding on future cases, even if the proposition constitutes a *sine qua non* of the actual decision: see *Slack v Leeds*
  [1923] 1 Ch 431 per Lord Sterndale @ 451 (*op.cit.*) and *Nixon v Attorney
  General* [1931] AC 184 HL per Viscount Dunedin @ 190 (*op.cit.*).

- If the authority has multiple *rationes*, is it distinguishable on the basis that
  the wrong ratio has been applied in the circumstances? A good example of
  fair criticism of an existing line of authority on this basis is to be found in
  the analysis by Lord Phillips of Worth Matravers MR in *Great Peace
  Shipping Ltd v Tsavliris Salvage Ltd* [2003] QB 679 of Lord Denning MR's
  approach in *Solle v Butcher* [1950] 1 KB 671 CA.

There are elements of the system of precedent which appear to have changed
over the last twenty years or so. Most recently this has crystallised in the
significant debate over tension between *stare decisis* and the freedom of final
courts of appeal to depart from and overrule previous decisions of their own
which they subsequently consider to have been wrong or no longer authoritative where the needs of society have changed in the meantime.[62] The
Judicial Committee of the Privy Council in *Lewis v Attorney General of
Jamaica*[63] and the House of Lords in *R v Kansal (No.2)*[64] raised for debate principles which should guide a court of final appeal in contemplation of
replacing its own wrongly decided precedents. The Appellate Committee has
considerations which do not apply to lesser tribunals – the policy decisions
that provide certainty to both the legal and wider community, especially in
commerce, property rights, and the provision of remedies for changing social
attitudes and needs.

The operation of precedent is not constant: despite extensive electronic data
retrieval and other support it remains impossible to guarantee that judges can
know every reported case. They still depend very largely on counsel for
citation of all relevant authority, and quite rightly so in view of the pressure
upon their time. Counsel are not infallible, particularly with the enormous
growth in the law itself, not merely law reporting. Sometimes this may result
in a judge arriving at a conclusion which might have been quite different if a

---

[62] See *Final Appellate Courts Overruling Their Own 'Wrong' Precedents: The Ongoing Search for Principle*
Prof. B V Harris (2002) 118 LQR 408.
[63] [2001] AC 50.
[64] [2001] 3 WLR 1562.

particular authority had been before him. That decision stands, and may be followed in other cases until, perhaps years later, the point comes before a higher court where the neglected authority is discovered and the clock must be put back.

The full impact on the common law of Convention rights and the Human Rights Act 1998 has yet to be seen, however, these are certain to have some impact on how judgments are decided, since potentially all common law rules and precedents are open to challenge. Lord Hope raised this spectre in *Kansal (No.2)*:[65]

> "As Lord Wilberforce observed in *Fitzleet Estates Ltd v Cherry* [1977] 1 WLR 1345, 1349D-E, the best way to resolve a question as to which there are two eminently possible views is by the considered majority opinion of the ultimate tribunal, and much more than mere doubts as to the correctness of that opinion are needed to justify departing from it. But the development of our jurisprudence on the Human Rights Act 1998 has only just begun. New problems are being revealed every week, if not every day. I believe that the interests of human rights law would not be well served if the House was to regard itself as bound by views expressed by the majority in a previous case about the meaning of provisions in that Act, if to adhere to those reasons would produce serious anomalies or other results which are plainly unsatisfactory: see *R v National Insurance Comr, Ex p Hudson* [1972] AC 944, 966, 993 per Lord Reid and Viscount Dilhorne."

If that is the way ahead the more pragmatic, perhaps idiosyncratic, decisions may have to be reigned in, with judges persuaded to start by contemplating the parties' rights. Although European Civil Law has no system of precedent or *stare decisis*, previous decisions interpreting the same legislation are used to show a consistent pattern of thought, even if not regarded as binding legal rules.

---

[65] *Op.cit.* @ 1578.

5.14

RATIO AND OBITER

It is of immense importance for both practitioner and judge to be precise about the *ratio* both in respect of the case being decided and any authority relied upon, since the hierarchy of precedent and the conclusiveness of a judgment both impact subsequently on substantive law. In its origin and essence a judgment is merely declaratory of rights, not creative of them. An action is a dispute as to the rights of the parties; a judgment is the decision of an arbitrator on the point at issue. However, by virtue of its conclusiveness a judgment comes to be regarded as creative of rights instead of declaratory of them: it is the substantive form of the rule of procedure that two actions cannot be brought for the same cause; the rule of procedure becomes trans-muted into the rule of substantive law that the right created by the judgment merges and destroys the right on which the judgment is founded.[66]

How to find the *ratio decidendi*, the application of legal criteria to the facts so giving rise to the legal reason for the decision, is a matter of first principle and not for discussion here. There are many cases where lawyers have accepted too general a formulation of the ratio – but reading a case is an exercise in inter-pretation; an exercise in exploring the range of possibilities. It is a matter of opinion. There is nothing wrong with you reading a case and thinking this is not really authority for the proposition stated in the textbook or even by the judge: all you have to do is prove that you are right. It is surprising how many times the cases cited in footnotes as authority for legal propositions turn out to be nothing of the sort.

It is unwise to presume that there is one and only one possible *ratio* to a case. In *Esso v C & E*[67] the House of Lords decided that where a decision is based upon two grounds, each forms part of the *ratio decidendi* of the case, so that a subsequent court is not entitled to single out one of the two and say it was *ratio* while the other was *obiter*: in *Jacobs* v *LCC* [1950] AC 361 HL Viscount Simonds[68] put it thus:

---

[66] See *The Superiority of Written Evidence* Salmond (1890) 6 LQR XXI 75 @ 84.
[67] [1976] 1 WLR 1.
[68] @ 369,370.

"It is not, I think, always easy to determine how far, when several issues are raised in a case and a determination of any one of them is decisive in favour of one or other of the parties, the observations upon other issues are to be regarded as obiter. That is the inevitable result of our system. For while it is the primary duty of a court of justice to dispense justice to litigants, it is its traditional role to do so by means of an exposition of the relevant law. Clearly such a system must be somewhat flexible, with the result that in some cases judges may be criticized for diverging into expositions which could by no means be regarded as relevant to the dispute between the parties; in others other critics may regret that an opportunity has been missed for making an oracular pronouncement upon some legal problem which has long vexed the profession. But, however this may be, there is in my opinion no justification for regarding as obiter dictum a reason given by a judge for his decision, because he has given another reason also. If it were a proper test to ask whether the decision would have been the same apart from the proposition alleged to be obiter, then a case which ex facie decided two things would decide nothing. A good illustration will be found in *London, Jewellers Ld.* v *Attenborough* [1934] 2 K.B. 206. In that case the determination of one of the issues depended on how far the Court of Appeal was bound by its previous decision in *Folkes* v *King* [1923] 1 K. B. 282. In the latter case the court had given two grounds for its decision, the second of which was that "where a man obtains possession with authority to sell, or to become the owner himself, and then sells, he cannot be treated as having obtained the goods by larceny by a trick." In the former case it was contended that, since there was another reason given for the decision, the second reason was obiter. But Greer L.J., from whose judgment I have taken the passage above cited, said in reference to the argument of counsel: "I cannot help feeling that if we were unhampered by authority there is much to be said for this proposition which commended itself to Swift J., and which commended itself to me in *Folkes* v *King* but that view is not open to us in view of the decision of the Court of Appeal in *Folkes* v *King*. In that case two reasons were given by all the members of the Court of Appeal for their decision and we are not entitled to pick out the first reason as the ratio decidendi and neglect the second, or to pick out the second reason as the ratio decidendi and neglect the first: we must take both as forming the ground of the judgment."

So also in *Cheater* v *Cater* Pickford L.J., after citing a passage from the judgment of Mellish L.J., in *Erskine* v *Adeane* said: "That is a distinct statement of the law and not a dictum. It is the second ground given by the Lord Justice for his judgment. If a judge states two grounds for his judgment and bases his decision upon both, neither of those grounds is a dictum.

The principle, which can be thus simply stated, is not always easy of application, particularly where the judgments of an appellate court consisting of more than one judge have to be considered."

Although strictly speaking, the *ratio decidendi* is limited to the point necessary for the decision, a lower court will be strongly inclined to follow the considered views of a higher court even though technically these can be described as *dicta*[69]. Judicial *dicta* may be irrelevant for deciding the case but may be relevant to some collateral matter which forms no part of the *ratio*. This is particularly true of opinions expressed in the speeches of the House of Lords which may intentionally be framed in wider terms than are necessary to decide the actual case so that they may serve as a guide to the future. If such expressions of opinion are noteworthy you should be conscious of the fact that *obiter dicta* are of different kinds and weight. There is a sharp distinction between carefully considered opinion on a point which has been argued by counsel, even though not necessary for the purpose of the judgment, and a mere casual or incautious expression made by the judge on a matter which has not been argued and therefore not been seriously considered by the Court: see per Lord Sterndale in *Slack* v *Leeds* [1923] 1 Ch 431 HL @ 451;

"Dicta are of different kinds and of varying degrees of weight. Sometimes they may be called almost casual expressions of opinion upon a point which has not been raised in the case, and is not really present to the judge's mind. Such dicta, though entitled to the respect due to the speaker, may fairly be disregarded by judges before whom the point has been raised and argued in a way to bring it under much fuller consideration. Some dicta however are of a different kind; they are, although not necessary for the decision of the case, deliberate expressions of opinion given after consideration upon a point clearly brought and argued before the Court. It is open no doubt to other judges to give decisions contrary to such dicta, but much greater weight attaches to them than to the former class. The dicta in *Dreyfus* v *Peruvian Guano Co.* are of the latter class. As I have shown the point was clearly brought before the Court and argued, and necessarily so, upon the view taken by Bowen L.J. There was ample opportunity for consideration of it, for though the judgment was not a reserved judgment the case had lasted over several days, being heard, according to the report, on November 21, 22, 23, 24, and December 2 and 3, and therefore there was ample time for consideration. Moreover it is quite plain from the judgment of Bowen L.J. that he had in fact given very careful consideration to the matter, and it is clear from his words that he had consulted."

---

[69] See *Learning Legal Rules Op.cit.* p.155.

and per Viscount Dunedin in *Nixon v Attorney General* [1931] AC 184 HL @ 190:

"When we come to authority, it seems to me that this case is most amply covered by authority. I agree that it is not covered by authority in this sense, that there is no actual judgment which binds this House, in which the precise point was the necessary and only point in the case. But the amount of learned opinion is quite overwhelming. In the first place, I do not think one must altogether forget the two old cases where the question was actually raised in absolute terms. No doubt they are not binding on this House, because they were decisions only of judges of first instance, but they were very learned judges, and their judgments have stood for many years without there being a single note of question against them in any case. Then, when one comes to more modern times, and to pronouncements in this House, there is the considered judgment of Lord Buckmaster, where, although the question may be said to be obiter to the case, it certainly was not obiter to the view that Lord Buckmaster took of the case, and accordingly he considered very carefully the series of statutes, and made that pronouncement which I have already quoted. Lord Loreburn gave an opinion to the same effect, although it was not so necessary in his view to consider that matter, but he went out of his way to say so. We have also the opinion of Lord Cave in the Privy Council and of Lord Reading in the Privy Council. That is really a very great array of authority, against which it would not be easy to go, unless there was some cogent reason for thinking that all those learned persons were wrong, and all that can be put against it is a casual expression, or, rather, I think, an incautious expression, made by the Master of the Rolls and Fletcher Moulton L.J. in *Lupton's* case [1912] 1 K. B. 107 where it was not necessary for them to consider the matter, and the matter was not argued, and I am afraid they slipped into that expression without exactly knowing what the result of it would be."

Since the late 17th century the courts have been offering definitions of what constitutes *obiter*. Lord Vaughan CJ described it as: "an opinion given in court, if not necessary to the judgment given of record, but that it might have been as well given if no such, or no contrary opinion, had been broached is no judicial opinion, no more than a *gratis dictum*."[70]

A test for *obiter*, which you might find useful, was developed in the 1890s:

i   frame carefully the supposed proposition of law;
ii   insert into the proposition a word reversing its meaning;

---

[70] *Bole v Horton* Vaugh. 360 @ 382.

iii consider whether, if the court had accepted this proposition as good, the decision would have been the same;

iv   if the answer is affirmative, however excellent the original proposition may be, the case is not a precedent for that proposition.[71]

---

[71] Wambaugh's *Study of Cases* (1894) (2nd edn) 17.

PART 6
ANALYSING JUDGMENTS:
TECHNIQUES FOR CRITICISM

6.1
CRITICISING A JUDGMENT FAIRLY

Successful appellate advocacy requires clear thinking, intellectual application and effective argument. In order to persuade an appellate tribunal that the judge below was wrong you must understand yourself why he was wrong, be able to demonstrate that fact with clarity, and withstand a rigorous testing of your contention. You must be prepared for reality testing by analogy and hypothesis, by reduction or expansion of your argument, and by purposive analysis; and you must be able to show the appellate tribunal that your criticism of the judge is fair, and that it is right or just that the appeal should succeed. You should be conscious not only of the judge's error, but also the merits of your client's own position. If you do not keep the merits firmly in mind, the court will. However great the error into which the first instance tribunal has fallen, whatever the departure from canon, if the merits are not with you, then your case will be found to be, on the facts, an aberration or an exception to the guiding principle, and whether intellectually sound or by sleight of hand, you will lose. You may win the argument, but you will lose the appeal.

Criticising a judgment fairly is the last stage of analytical reading. It involves giving an exacting consideration to the text and calls for a five stage process:

1   Reading actively

2   Developing a close understanding

3   Making a critical judgment

4   Understanding why you disagree

5   Forming a structured reply.

Active reading entails not blandly accepting what is being said. It requires an alertness in which the reader is prepared to challenge the writer to persuade him of the correctness of his position. It is unlike a passive operation in which information is absorbed without applying any critical faculty. You should remember that while grammatical and logical skill in writing clearly and intelligibly has merit in itself, the aim of a judgment is also to convince or persuade. The judge may use rhetorical or literary techniques, or the plainest of common language. Whatever the devices, they are intended to justify his findings. Your task is to react critically to the attempt to persuade.

The writer seeks to achieve intelligibility in his work and to convey understanding to his reader. The lawyer must achieve understanding before he can properly criticise. It may be that on occasion your judge is so prolix or diffuse that you have to strip away verbiage in order to search for understanding, but understand you must. As Adler suggests[1] you must be able to say with reasonable certainty "I understand" before you can say "I agree", "I disagree" or "I suspend judgment". These three remarks exhaust all the critical positions you can take. However please bear in mind that criticism does not mean merely to disagree. To agree is just as much an exercise of critical judgment as disagreement. Suspending judgment is also an act of criticism: it is taking a position that something has not been shown or proven, which is highly pertinent to forensic analysis.

You must understand why you disagree, because your disagreement must be purposive if it is to enable you to appeal successfully. What is at stake is persuading an appellate tribunal that the basis of the disagreement – or the criticism of the judge's judgment – is sufficiently causative or relevant or important first that the appeal should be permitted to be heard, and second, to succeed. An appeal is a futile agitation unless undertaken with the hope that it may either succeed before the court or at least lead to the resolution of an issue between the parties. Disagreement for its own sake is not enough: the costs regime is designed to deter criticism of judicial performance unless it not only has merit but will also be of practical significance.

Forming a structured reply will enable you to marshal your thought processes at the earliest stage, perhaps well before you are called upon to advise or settle a notice of appeal and skeleton argument in support. Once you have identified the basis for your criticism you need to formulate an argument that enables the appellate tribunal to understand not only why the judge's finding is wrong, but also why your client's desired outcome is to be preferred.

---

[1] *Op. cit.* p. 142.

6.2
ANALYSING YOUR DISAGREEMENT OBJECTIVELY

You have concluded that the judgment may properly and fairly be criticised. Next try and consider the position objectively as an outsider, in this case as the appellate tribunal, would. This is no doubt difficult in view of the two subjective opening positions. You believe that the judge was wrong. However, the appellate tribunal will instinctively start from a defensive point of view, wishing to protect the reputation and dignity of the court under attack, unless by some oversight or procedural defect it is fairly obvious that no reasonable tribunal could have come to the conclusion being appealed against. Taking a step back and making sure that you believe your criticism of the judge is reasonable, and that you are not just acting disputatiously or contentiously, may overcome this difficulty.

Consider whether the substance of your criticism concerns genuine knowledge, and not mere personal opinion. If the latter, then for the most part such disagreements may be more apparent than real. If the criticism has real substance it must concern genuine issues of fact and reason.

6.3
DISTINGUISHING BETWEEN KNOWLEDGE AND OPINION

If the judge does not provide reasoning or support for his propositions they can properly be treated as personal opinions only on his part. While it is facile to say that all judgments are only the personal opinion of the judge, for appellate purposes it is vitally important to distinguish between the reasoned statement of knowledge and the flat expression of personal opinion. Critical obligations should be taken seriously: the practitioner must do more than make judgments of agreement and disagreement. He must have adequate reasons for doing so which can be justified in fact or law.

In this respect you must realise and accept that most knowledge is not absolute. Knowledge consist of opinions which can be defended, opinions for which there is evidence of one kind or another. Knowledge in this sense is something we can convince others of what we know. Mere opinion, on the other hand, is unsupported judgment. What is required is evidence or reason for a statement over and above personal feeling or prejudice: objective evidence that other reasonable men are likely to accept.[2] In dealing with an appellate tribunal you will be engaged in intelligent controversy and challenged not only to carry your own argument but also to deal with the arguments of the tribunal itself.

---

[2] See Adler *op. cit.* pp.149, 150.

6.4

THE FOCUS OF YOUR CRITICISM

The judge is making judgments about the world in which we live in the context of the facts of the case. His findings as to the facts in dispute give us knowledge or tell us what things exist, the way they behave and what should be done. He can be either right or wrong. His position is justified only to the extent that he says what is probable in the light of the evidence; were that not so it may be contended that his conclusion is unfounded.

Once again, much turns on your understanding with precision the judge's meaning, otherwise your disagreement may be irrelevant: an error of under-standing in what he is saying may render the opposite argument without merit. If your criticism is founded upon a misapprehension, the appellate process will be an expensive failure. Issues about matters of fact or policy – the way things are or should be – are real only when they are based upon a common understanding of what is being said. Agreement about the use of words is an indispensable condition for genuine agreement or disagreement about the facts under discussion.[3] You must therefore ensure, as objectively as possible, that there is a real and significant issue at stake which can be readily identified, and is irresolvable with the mechanism of an appeal.

---

[3] *Ibid* p. 153.

6.5

THE MECHANICS OF FAIR CRITICISM

There are principally four ways in which a judgment can be adversely but fairly criticised: that the judge was uninformed; that he was misinformed; that his approach was illogical in the sense that his reasoning was not cogent; or that his analysis of either the facts or the law was not complete. These four categories are not exhaustive, but they cover most points that are likely to arise. Nor are the defects they describe mutually exclusive.

You cannot mount a sound challenge without being definite and precise about the respect in which the judgment is uninformed or misinformed or illogical, since it is most unlikely that judges of the calibre engaged in our courts and tribunals will be uninformed and misinformed about everything, or else totally illogical.

UNINFORMED:

The judge lacks some piece of knowledge that is relevant to the problem he is trying to solve. You must yourself be able to state a piece of knowledge or information missing, show its relevance, and show how the conclusion would be different. This is often reflected in such criticism by the Court of Appeal as that given by Scott Baker J in *In re Rhondda Waste Disposal Ltd:*[4]

> "In my judgment the judge was in error in the exercise of his discretion. He should not have regarded the interests of the creditors of the company as trumping all other considerations. He failed to take into account and give due weight to the evidence of Mr Weare. Furthermore, in the event of conviction, there is a statutory obligation on the court fixing the amount of any fine to take account of all the circumstances including the financial circumstances of the company: see section 18(3) of the Criminal Justice Act 1991.

---

[4] [2001] Ch 57 CA per @ 71[42].

43 I consider there were compelling reasons why leave should have been given in this case. The purpose of licensing is to ensure that the disposal of controlled waste does not give rise to: (i) pollution of the environment; (ii) harm to human health and; (iii) serious detriment to the amenities of the locality."

Equally the trial judge's analysis of law may be called into question, as did Lord Denning MR here in *Heywood* v *Wellers*:[5]

'Now I think the judge was in error in thinking that the solicitors were entitled to recover any costs at all. There are two reasons. In the first place, the contract of the solicitors was an entire contract which they were bound to carry on to the end; and, not having done so, they were not entitled to any costs: see *Underwood, Son & Piper* v *Lewis* [1894] 2 Q.B. 306. The law as to *entire* contract was put vividly by Sir George Jessel M.R., in *In re Hall & Barker* (1878) 9 Ch.D. 538, 545:

"If a man engages to carry a box of cigars from London to Birmingham, it is an entire contract, and he cannot throw the cigars out of the carriage half-way there, and ask for half the money; or if a shoemaker agrees to make a pair of shoes, he cannot offer you one shoe and ask you to pay one half the price."

In the second place, the work which they did do was useless. It did nothing to forward the object which the client had in view. It did nothing to protect her from molestation. It being thus useless, they can recover nothing for it: see *Hill* v *Featherstonhaugh* (1831) 7 Bing. 569, when Tudai C.J. said, at pp. 571–572:

"... if an attorney, through inadvertence or inexperience, – for I impute no improper motive to the plaintiff – incurs trouble which is useless to his client, he cannot make it a subject of remuneration... could a bricklayer, who had placed a wall in such a position as to be liable to fall, charge his employer for such an erection?"

Clearly not. So the solicitors were entitled to nothing for costs: and Mrs. Heywood could recover the £175 as money paid on a consideration which had wholly failed. She was, therefore, entitled to recover it as of right."

---

[5] [1976] QB 446 @ 458

MISINFORMED

Here he asserts that which is not the case, i.e. the judge makes findings or assertions contrary to fact. The judgment proposes as true or more probable that which is in fact false or less probable; it is based on a claim to have knowledge he does not possess. This was the focus of criticism by Lord Justice Stocker in the Court of Appeal of the trial judge in one of the actions arising out the Hillsborough disaster:

> "To summarise, in my view, the law is that, save in exceptional circumstances, only those within the parent/spouse relationship can recover damages for psychiatric shock sustained by a plaintiff not himself involved as a victim. This defines the category. The exceptions considered on a case to case basis are limited to relatives who meet the criteria of that relationship and who are present at the scene or its immediate aftermath. What has to be foreseeable is that someone may be present at the scene or its immediate aftermath who possesses that love and affection which a parent/spouse is assumed to possess, even if in fact that relative is less closely related to the victim than a parent or spouse. It does not seem to me that such a formulation causes any particular difficulty – it is a slight reformulation of the test of foreseeability to meet the cases referred to by Lord Wilberforce, not any change or addition to what has to be foreseeable in the case of a parent/spouse who suffers psychiatric injury by shock. The judge found that in the case before him brother and sister were entitled to recover. He did so, if I correctly interpret his judgment, by reference to the circumstances of the Hillsborough disaster and by the relationship which might be expected in most cases between brother and sister. He did not carry out any close scrutiny by reference to the love and affection in fact to be attributed to them, having regard in particular to any care (in the sense of custody or maintenance) which they had performed. It may be that had such a scrutiny been carried out, the facts might have entitled them to recover damages and the extension in their favour be justified under the principles enunciated by Lord Wilberforce. I therefore consider that the judge was in error in holding that in the circumstances of the case before him he could regard the brothers and sisters as within the relationship which would entitle them to claim damages."[6]

This kind of defect is only relevant if it is causative in the sense that it affects the judge's conclusions and ultimate position; see, for example, the child abduction case *B. v B.*:[7]

---

[6] *Alcock* v *Chief Constable of South Yorkshire* [1992] 1 AC 310 CA @ 379.
[7] [1993] Fam 32 per Sir Stephen Brown P @ 38.

"In support of the judge's finding that the removal was not unlawful, Mr. Warnock for the mother submits that the court should apply a strict and restricted interpretation of the term "rights of custody." Since the court had ordered interim custody in favour of the mother (subject to access by the father pending the substantive hearing) there could be no right of custody in any person or body other than the mother. Therefore, he says, she was not in breach of any right vested in the husband, or, indeed, in the court when she removed the child on 3 July 1991.

I find that submission unacceptable. In my view this was the plainest example of an unlawful removal. The mother herself appears to have thought so, for she later stated that she regretted having taken that step at that time. It is suggested that she did not appreciate the legal position, although she was in receipt of legal advice at the time. It seems to me that the court itself had a right of custody at this time in the sense that it had the right to determine the child's place of residence, and it was in breach of that right that the mother removed the child from its place of habitual residence. I should say that there has never been any issue as to the fact that the child's habitual residence was at all material time in Ontario. Accordingly, I am of the view that the judge was in error when he decided that the removal of the child was not unlawful."

You must be able to argue the truth or greater probability of a position contrary to that of the judge. It should follow as a matter of logic that whenever he is misinformed in one respect, he will also be uninformed in the same respect.

ILLOGICAL

The judge has committed a fallacy in reasoning. This problem generally stems from two sources. Either the judge has fallen into the trap of *non sequitor*, where what is drawn as a conclusion simply does not follow from the reasons offered, or that of inconsistency, where two things he has tried to say are incompatible. To make either criticism you must be able to show the precise respect in which the judge's argument lacks cogency. The judge may have fail to draw the conclusions that the evidence or principles imply: the criticism derives not from poor evidence but from reasoning poorly from good grounds, and in that sense the judgment can also be impeached as being uninformed.

In *The Miraflores and The Abadesa*,[8] a shipping case involving a collision, Winn LJ in the Court of Appeal found that he could not support the trial judge's approach which he considered illogical:

---

[8] [1966] P 18 @ 35 *et seq.*

"In the incident which gave rise to this action there were two events, separate in space and time, though not widely separate in either of those elements. The collision between the *Abadesa* and the *Miraflores* was one of those events; the other, partially but not inevitably consequential upon it, was the grounding of the *George Livanos*. Each event was the subject of a separate action: Folio 218 in respect of the grounding, and Folio 228 in respect of the collision. Those actions were heard together. Of the two events, the earlier in point of time, the collision, was far and away the more serious, and it was in every respect natural that Hewson J. should have applied his mind first to determining the respective proportions of fault for that collision to be attributed to the two ships involved in it. He made such a determination, and assessed the *Abadesa* as two-thirds to blame and the *Miraflores* as one-third to blame. That was an assessment of fault in respect of the collision.

He then turned to a consideration of the causes or faults which produced the grounding of the *George Livanos*. He held that the *George Livanos* had herself been 50 per cent. to blame for going aground, and had to that extent been the author of her own misfortune and damage. He expressed that determination thus: "In action Folio 218 I propose to treat the negligence leading to the collision ... as one unit, and the negligence of the *George Livanos* as another." It seems to me that, in so determining, Hewson J. was adopting a mental process of quasi-personification of the collision itself, and that what he was saying when he declared the *George Livanos* to be 50 per cent. responsible for having gone aground was that half the cause of the grounding had been the collision and half the fault or faults of the *George Livanos* in respect of her navigation preceding the grounding. He said: "In action Folio 218 I find it impossible to distinguish between the degrees of fault between the two units." Save in so far as one of those units comprised two ships and the other only one, he did not anywhere in his judgment distinguish, in respect specifically of the grounding, the respective faults of the three individual ships involved.

With the utmost respect to Hewson J. which I sincerely entertain for any view of his, I cannot help thinking that in this respect he fell into a logical fallacy. Since the collision was part of the causation of the grounding, the whole of the responsibility for that consequence of the collision, as well as for the collision, has to be attributed to the respective vessels by whose fault the collision and that consequence of it were caused. As I see it, Hewson J. did not apportion at all one-half of the responsibility for producing the grounding. It having already been determined that the responsibility for producing the collision rested as to $66^2/_3$ per cent. upon the *Abadesa,* and to $33^1/_3$ per cent. upon the *Miraflores,* the reasoning might properly proceed on one or other of two parallel lines: either (1) the 50 per cent. residue over and above the fault of the *George Livanos* for the occurrence of the grounding, that is, 50 per cent. of the responsibility for that event, should be distributed equally upon each of the other two vessels so as to add 25 per cent. of responsibility for the grounding and the damage caused thereby to the respective shares of responsibility for the collision; or (2) the share of the same 50 per cent. responsibility for the grounding might be attributed to the *Abadesa* and the *Miraflores* in the same proportions precisely as those fixed in respect of the collision, so as to produce an assessment of $66^2/_3$ per cent. of 50 per cent., that is, $33^1/_3$ per cent. in respect of the grounding damage against the *Abadesa,* and, by parity of reasoning, $16^2/_3$ per cent. (that is, $33^1/_3$ per cent. of 50 per cent.) in respect of the grounding damage against the *Miraflores.*

Responsibility for an event does not terminate when the event occurs, but comprises liability for consequences flowing from the event. By such a method as I have suggested, it seems to me that there is achieved what is not achieved by Hewson J.'s approach: an assessment in respect of each ship of the overall responsibility for the occurrence of the double event of the collision and the partially consequential grounding. For the collision, of course, the *George Livanos* bore no responsibility. I venture to think that Hewson J. was led by the approach which he adopted to lay too much stress upon causation or causative potency and too little upon elements of blame to which due regard must be had; cf. *The British Aviator* et passim."

Once again, you are concerned with the respective defect only to the extent that major conclusions are affected by it, or perhaps by the cumulative effect of such defects. For our purposes a judgment may safely lack cogency in irrelevant respects. This class of criticism requires penetrative reading because the defects are usually well concealed.

INCOMPLETENESS

The basis of this critique is to say the judge

- has not solved all the problems he started with; or

- he has not made use of all the available material; or

- he did not see all the ramifications and implications; or

- he has failed to make all the distinctions relevant to his task.

This might derive from his erroneous acceptance of facts which should be challenged, or it might be an incomplete analysis of thinking because it makes assumptions or fails to make assumptions: an example is to be found in the criticism of an arbitration award in *Drake Insurance Plc* v *Provident Insurance Plc*[9] (CA):

> "In my judgment, the judge was in error in concluding that there was no evidence to suggest that the no fault status of the prior accident would have emerged. Until 7 February 1997 Provident had said nothing to suggest that the disclosure of the fault accident had anything to do with its claim to avoid the policy. When, however, the connection with the status of that accident was first made in Mr Shaw's letter of that date, Dr Singh's next communication with Provident, his letter to the chief executive dated 5 March 1997, straightway pointed out that the accident had been a no fault one. It was the point he made in his first numbered paragraph, after the words: "Mr Shaw did not mention in our telephone conversation any of the other points raised in his letter dated 6 February 1997, if he had I certainly would have corrected his misunderstandings..."
>
> **61** Dr Singh kept that point well in view, for instance in his letter in reply to the arbitrator. It was a great pity that in his award the arbitrator paid no attention whatsoever to this factor."

---

[9] [2003] EWCA Civ 1834; [2004] QB 601 per Rix LJ @ 621.

6.6

THE STRUCTURED CRITIQUE

In preparing your structured reply undertake the following process:

- Make a list outlining all the problems which the judge is trying to solve. The last step of interpretation is to know which of these problems the judge solved and which he did not.

- Assess in respect of those problems he failed to solve, whether these impact on your client's position as a whole.

- If so, identify the basis of the omission in respect of each relevant fact or consequence omitted.

- If not (or in addition), consider in respect of the problems which the judge did solve, how satisfactory the solutions are.

- Identify those solutions which are to be the subject of complaint, classifying them as uninformed, misinformed or illogical.

PART 7
WRITING JUDGMENTS, DECISIONS AND AWARDS

"Litigants want judgments, not rhetoric, so that they can get on with their lives ..."

Judge Wald, District of Columbia Circuit[1]

---

[1] (1995) 62 U.Chi.LR p.1385.

7.1

DELIVERING AND WRITING JUDGMENTS

Down to the chancellorship of Lord Lyndhurst in the 1830s the concept of a reserved written judgment was virtually unknown, even in the higher courts.[2] Judgments are still for the most part given, and encouraged to be given, *ex tempore* at the conclusion of argument, as this has advantages both for the parties and the judges themselves: the parties have the immediacy of a result; reasoning is directed very much to the facts, as it should be at first instance; judgments are invariably shorter and more simple; and the parties are saved the expense of an adjourned hearing. The judge has the benefit of addressing matters while fresh in his mind, and in particular his perception of the witnesses; he can move directly on to questions of costs, interest and drafting any order consequent upon the judgment; he can conclude a unit of business. This is not an unimportant factor in a system where neither full- nor part-time judges receive any extra payment for preparing reserved written judgments.

This is not to say that the judge should rush to judgment, since he should be clear in his mind as to what he is going to decide, and be ready to do so; there is always a danger that a hurried judgment will omit something of importance and lead either to an appeal or at least impart a feeling of real injustice in the losing party. Retirement for a few minutes, over a short adjournment, or overnight if at the end of a long sitting day may help clear the judge's mind and render the judgment more succinct.

The reserved judgment has the benefit of enabling the judge to come to terms with complex issues of fact and law, and to deal with lengthy bodies of evidence or the close examination of a copious amount of documents. The judge can take as much time as he needs over the decision; he can ensure that nothing is omitted, that each issue is resolved, and his reasoning is correct; he may hone and perfect what he wishes to say, select his language more carefully and prepare and edit drafts before delivery. If he dictates his judgments he will

---

[2] See *The Form and Language of Judicial Opinions* Lord Roger op.cit. 232.

have the opportunity of correcting grammatical errors and inconsistencies of which he might otherwise be unaware until asked to approve a court transcript to be used for the purpose of an appeal. If he uses a word processing package himself, he can scrutinise his own spelling and grammar at leisure.

Reserving judgment, and in particular reserving first instance decisions on any regular basis, will put a judge under pressure. The longer he leaves it the greater will be the difficulty in constructing it. Irrespective of a detailed note it is likely that any independent memory and 'feel' for the case will rapidly deteriorate. During the hearing the judge is required to exhibit an intensity of concentration, which, as time passes, will often be impossible to reproduce. It is no answer for a judge to rely on a recording service such as 'Livenote' if he has lost the impression conveyed by the witness at the time. Moreover delay between the close of evidence and the delivery of judgment or award has become a matter of considerable scrutiny by the Privy Council,[3] the Court of Appeal[4] and appellate tribunals.[5] It gives rise to the possibility of a decision (or part of it) being rendered unsafe. The old common law adage of justice delayed being justice denied is reflected substantively in the European Convention on Human Rights, as the House of Lords has made clear:

"the right in Article 6 (1) to a determination within a reasonable time is an independent right, and that it is to be distinguished from the Article 6 (1) right to a fair trial".[6]

---

[3] *Cobham* v *Frett* [2001] 1 WLR 1775 per Lord Scott of Foscote at 1783–4.

[4] *Gardiner Fire Ltd* v *Jones* (unrep) 20 October 1998 CA; *Keith Davy (Crantock)* v *Ibatex Ltd* [2001] EWCA Civ. 740 per Tuckey LJ at para [31]; *Goose* v *Wilson Sandford & Co* The Times, 19 February 1998; *Times Newspapers Ltd* v *Singh & Choudry* (unrep) 17 December 1999; Court of Appeal (Civil Division) transcript No 2156 of 1999.

[5] *Kwamin* v *Abbey National Plc* (unrep.) EAT 2nd March 2004 UKEAT/0564/03 and three consolidated appeals; *Chinyanga* v *Buffer Bear Ltd* (unrep) 8 May 2003 EAT (EAT/0300/02); *The Governors of Warwick Park School and Others* v *Hazlehurst and Others* (unrep) EAT 19 February 2001 (EAT/540/99); *Barker and Others* v *The Home Office* (unrep) 7 August 2002 (EAT804/01).

[6] *Porter v Magill* [2002] 2 AC 357 per Lord Hope @ para [108]; see also *Obasa* v *United Kingdom* [2003] All ER (D) 84 (Jan).

7.2
PREPARATION

Merely because a judgment is delivered ex *tempore* that is not an indication that the judge has undertaken no preparation: quite the reverse. Only highly experienced members of the judiciary, at whatever level, are able to deliver a truly 'off the cuff' performance. It comes naturally to very few. A successful judgment is one that is:

- Unimpeachable;

- Decisive;

- Addresses the precise issues the parties wish to be resolved;

- Cogent;

- Well-reasoned;

- Satisfies even the loser that he has been met with a fair, albeit disappointing decision.

The key is preparation.

Time permitting, pre-reading the statements of case, counsel's skeleton arguments, and the core witness statements and documents will enable the judge to have identified the relevant facts and principal issues before even going into court. An adequate but not overly fulsome chronology is probably the most important tool in preparing and delivering a judgment ex *tempore*. If that provided by the parties is inadequate, a judge would do well to prepare his own, either prior to or during the course of the hearing as the material facts emerge. For the purpose of creating a structured judgment with ease, it is the chronology that forms a skeleton on which the findings of fact can be grown. Unquestionably much of the early part of a judgment can be written before the case has been concluded, certainly before the facts have been decided. Judges who use a formulaic approach to the structure of their judgments may have more than half of what they will eventually say prepared before closing arguments are made.

If the time is not available for any extensive pre-reading beyond the statements of case and written submissions, the judge should decide quickly whether the skeleton arguments submitted are sufficiently reliable and comprehensive to use as an *aide memoire* for the purpose of setting out the facts and issues to be decided directly in the judgment. If not he will jot down matters that he wants to include in his judgment as the hearing progresses. Throughout the trial experienced judges not only mark up important passages in the evidence but will make marginal notes, and often cross reference matters to a separate sheet of paper where they have begun to formulate the structure of the judgment, much of which will afterwards be read straight from the judge's notebook. This will almost always be true of fast track claims.

7.3
JUDGMENT IN THE LOWER COURTS

The quality of a judgment depends on the time available to prepare and deliver it. The pressure of business in the lower courts, with small value and therefore higher relative cost claims, keeps the judge's time at a premium. Whatever the pressure of time Article 6 requires that all decisions, including the exercise of a discretion, be reasoned and therefore justifiable.[7] Applications for permission to appeal and interim procedural applications almost always require *ex tempore* decisions where the district judge or master must give a clear explanation to the litigant, particularly where the effect of the decision is to terminate a claim or a defence.

The general framework for a judgment in the lower courts will be the same for both an *ex tempore* and a reserved judgment. Whilst the broad approach will be no different, a reserved judgment is likely to set out more clearly defined issues and more detailed findings than a judgment in the same case given *ex tempore*, where there is a tendency to run issues together more, and to avoid dealing with minor events. Not only is there a danger of missing issues, but it is tempting for the judge to jump into findings without analysing the evidence on discrete issues.

Nonetheless at the lowest level, the judge should expect always to deliver his judgment *ex tempore*. If time does permit it pays to write the whole judgment out and read it through to make sure it sounds alright: preparation is as much a time-saving device as an intellectual exercise. If he pre-reads, the judge can prepare the first stages of judgment before going into court, take his facts from the skeleton, and fill in the evidence and his conclusions. This preparation enables the judge to concentrate on the conflicting submissions. If he uses a laptop computer to take his notes of evidence he will usually put passages straight into the judgment. Where necessary he will take the time to make a cross-reference to arguments in the skeleton, the authorities and the practice

---

[7] *Porter* v *McGill op. cit.* per Lord Hope @ [108].

books. Except for the burden of proof and key principles, at this level he need not worry unduly about the law: judges at first instance in the lower courts are neither required nor do they wish to make general statements about law.

7.4
JUDICIAL TRAINING

The law imposes no specific requirements upon the structure and content of civil judgments. Unlike the formulaic approach of the superior courts of the United States, the European Court and the ECHR, and certain tribunal awards, there are no set rules, no practice directions and no guidance from the senior judges, except occasional approbation expressed on appeal. A judge is free to choose both the form and the language in which his opinion is expressed. Every judge has his or her own approach and preferences to the form and organisation of the judgment, the use and abuse of language, units of writing and literary technique. Not only that, but the training of judges in judgment writing is both limited and of comparatively recent origin.

The Judicial Studies Board,[8] which provides training and instruction for all full-time and part-time judges in the skills necessary to be a judge, was founded only in 1979. It has an advisory role in the training of lay magistrates and of chairmen and members of tribunals. An essential element of the philosophy of the JSB is that the training of judges and magistrates is under judicial control and directions.[9]

In hindsight it seems extraordinary that, until well into the 1990s, deputy High Court judges sat without any form of induction or training. The reason being (presumably), that senior civil practitioners of the type selected could move seamlessly from providing an opinion to a party, to delivering it from the bench. Formal training in compiling and delivering judgments is still relatively in its infancy. During the late 1980s and early 1990s, recorders and district judges were provided at either their county court or family court induction course with a lecture by a sitting judge on how to structure judgments as part of the training devoted to the role of the county court judge. From 1998 that part of the Judicial Studies Board Civil Induction Course was supplemented by the addition of a training exercise in syndicate form in which candidates prepared a draft judgment overnight for discussion with an

---

[8] "JSB".
[9] See JSB website.

experienced civil judge the following morning. That remains the totality of the training given in judgment writing. In fairness it is right to say that the majority of those attending the course are familiar with judgments and the giving of reasoned opinions from many years of private practice.

In the higher courts the JSB provides regular training seminars, perhaps every six months, to both puisne judges and members of the Court of Appeal. At the time of writing the most recent seminar on judgment writing was given in October 2002, and again was based on a syndicate exercise. It is thought that the form of judgments delivered in the High Court have been more consistent since.

The JSB produces guidelines on delivering judgment in its current *Civil Bench Book*[10] but makes the point that "there is no 'bombproof' formula or JSB 'house style' and the following is not meant to suggest that there is". In fact the instructions given are so little in scope that, by kind permission, it is worth reproducing them in their entirety here:

"10.4 Structure of the judgment

No two judgments are alike, but it is helpful if you can adopt a general structure which will help you marshal your thoughts and make what you say easier to assimilate.

a) Begin by stating the nature of the claim or application. Identify the parties, and summarise the question(s) that you have to decide. This is frequently done in a fairly conventional and obvious format.

b) Next, summarise the relevant facts. Tell the story as far as possible in chronological order. Make sure that you clearly identify which facts are agreed and which facts are significantly in contention. Try to deal with the agreed facts as early as possible in your narrative, as this will clarify matters later on

c) Summarise the relevant law (should this be appropriate). Obviously where there is no issue as to the law and the matter turns on disputed fact, it may not be necessary to do this, although occasionally it will be helpful to do so. If there has been a dispute as to the law, refer to the main authorities relied on by the parties, together with the references. Wherever possible avoid having to quote from judgments and getting too 'academic' – usually the case name, reference and proposition it supports should be sufficient. If you do feel compelled to quote from the case, keep it short

---

[10] August, 2001 edn.

and identify the relevant passage by page and paragraph number wherever possible.

d) Briefly set out the material issues and main arguments on each side. Take care to ensure that you have summarised the principal submissions of the unsuccessful party, in order to demonstrate that you have understood them and taken them into account. This will also be helpful in the event that the Court of Appeal has ultimately to consider the matter.

e) Make your essential findings of fact, and rulings on any disputed points of law. Ensure that when you do make findings of fact, you do so clearly. Provided you formulate your findings with care, and there is some credible evidence to support them, it will be very difficult for them to be successfully appealed. If at all possible, avoid having to make remarks which express (or imply) moral censure, excessive criticism, or emotion. Also avoid appearing pompous or patronising. If it is essential to brand someone a liar, then of course do not shrink from doing so, but otherwise attempt to be as diplomatic as possible. Most of the time it will be sufficient to use a variation of 'I prefer the recollection of Mr Bloggs', or 'Although I am not suggesting that Mr Bloggs is trying deliberately to mislead the court, I am nevertheless satisfied that he is wrong when he says...' Be careful not to express criticism in terms which may, in the cold light of objective hindsight, appear insensitive.

If you have received particular help from the advocates, or if they have conducted the case efficiently and helpfully, by all means say so. Do not however, praise the conduct of one party and not the other, unless it can be done in a context which may not be seen as a slur on the other. Likewise, if a party to the action has been truthful and helpful, pay tribute to that – particularly if you are going to decide against that person notwithstanding.

Make your rulings on law as succinct as possible, whilst always ensuring that no one can subsequently criticise you for failing to set out our reasoning.

At the same time, do not let sensitivity or diplomacy weaken your decision so that it appears weak. Be firm in your decisions and in the way in which you give them. Try not to use phrases like 'this difficult case' unless you really have found it difficult, or you will have difficulty in resisting an application for permission to appeal, having encouraged the losing party (and his lawyers) to think that the case was of sufficient complexity to warrant taking it further. Likewise, unless it is one of those rare cases in which the phrase is justified, try not to give judgment 'with regret', even if you are trying to spare someone's feelings. It detracts from your authority, and encourages dissatisfaction.

f) Make sure that you decide all necessary matters. If you have to exercise a discretion, make sure that you say so, do so, and identify all the factors (for and against) which you have taken into account in carrying out the balancing exercise."

From this general, and current guidance can be drawn five guiding principles to ensure the delivery of a successful judgment:

1   Be firm.
2   Be comprehensive.
3   Be diplomatic.
4   Be clear.
5   Be succinct.

In the course of JSB lectures over the years[11] other particular advice has been given to new appointees as set out below.

ON FINDING FACTS

Although a judge should be quite short about the evidence it is very important that the facts be found in full. He must deal with direct evidence of the primary facts, and state what inferences are to be drawn from his findings on the secondary facts: he must grapple with them, especially if they are in dispute. The judge should indicate separately which are primary and which secondary findings of fact.

ON ADDRESSING THE LOSER

The judge will be more comfortable in giving judgment if during the trial he treats each party as the potential loser: in the judgment his remarks should primarily be addressed to the losing party, since he will need reasons put in simple terms. Even if he is disappointed, the loser needs to go away satisfied that justice has been done. In particular he needs to know the reasons why the evidence of witnesses adduced for the losing party is not being accepted, and that the judge has taken into account all of the arguments addressed on his behalf.

---

[11] In particular 'Judgments and the Role of Judge in the County Court' Lord Justice Scott, County Court Induction Course, April, 1992; 'Giving Judgment' HH Judge Marr-Johnson, County Court Induction Course, September, 1998.

ON THE TASK IN HAND

It is essential to reach a decision before giving reasons. Occasionally a judge will have no clear view until he analyses his findings, weighs them up, and applies the burden of proof and the law. Since the judge has to express reasons for his findings, he must know what those reasons are – the factors he taken into account; those which bear upon the exercise of any discretion; and why his discretion is being exercised in a particular way. It is to feel confident in his understanding that the judge is encouraged to adjourn (but not reserve) for as long as he needs.

ON THE ISSUE OF CREDIBILITY

Issues of credibility must be addressed; they can not be left floating around at the end of the trial. If evidence is simply unreliable or untruthful the judge should not be mealy-mouthed about it. He should say in terms, "I don't believe X or Y", and make clear why he rejects the evidence. He should not indicate any difficulty he may have had in coming to a decision on credibility. The judge should not go out of his way merely to brand someone a liar, unless he is so finding in a fraud case, and he may modify his position by his choice of language: he may say, "I prefer the evidence of X to Y"; or "I don't accept Y's evidence except where it is supported by documents or other oral evidence" or "where oral evidence contradicts a document, I prefer the contents of the document." The language used needs to be sufficient to indicate what is the judge's preferred version of events.

ON THE USE OF LANGUAGE

The judge ought to be able to encapsulate the case in a few sentences. Although he may choose both his use of language and literary techniques, he should avoid headline-catching phrases: the press love it; litigants hate it. Nor should he write with one eye on how it will be viewed in the Court of Appeal. He must not lose sight of the basic fact that his judgment is merely a decision with reasons for it. He makes findings and grants relief without condemnation or admonition. He may use the costs regime for that!

7.5
PERSONAL VIEWS ON FRAMEWORK

Judges interviewed for this book have offered their own personal views on the framework or structure that best suits the majority of the cases in which they give judgment. Distilling this information shows the emergence of a pattern which may be appropriate to a typical type of hearing.

CIVIL FASTTRACK

- Describe the case briefly, referring to the statements of case.
- State what issues are in contention.
- Set out the history that relates to the relevant issues.
- Identify what parts of the history are not in dispute.
- Resolve the issues of fact in dispute.
- State the law as you find it, dealing with the law only shortly.
- Apply the law to the facts.
- Give judgment on the facts as found.

FAMILY CASES

- Set out the agreed facts and non-contentious background.
- Identify what material the Court has read, and from whom it has heard.
- Précis the opposing submission, setting out the case for both applicant and respondent.
- Deal with the law.
- Make value judgments: what evidence is preferred, and why.
- Identify and order the appropriate relief.

MASTER'S OR DISTRICT JUDGE'S APPLICATION

- Introduction: Take the issues from the application notice.

- Deal very briefly with the claim by encapsulating the statements of case.

- Find the facts as appropriate on the available evidence.

- Having found the facts, look at the law.

- Balance the submissions for each party; (if there is a litigant in person deal with the crucial argument rather than compare submissions).

- Apply the legal test to the points in contention.

- Make findings and give reasons.

HIGH COURT TRIAL

- Introduction – what the claim is for – give a brief non-contentious history.

- Define the issues – refer to statements of case and argument.

- Set out the scope of the present hearing.

- Address the relevant evidence and legal consequences of each issue, summarising the case for either side.

- Make relevant findings of fact.

- Apply the law to remedies sought.

- Conclusion.

In some cases a formulaic approach is readily apparent, a good example being the judgment of Mr Justice Jackson in R. v *Secretary of State for the Home Department ex p. Wright*:[12]

"1. MR JUSTICE JACKSON: This judgment is in nine parts, namely:

Part 1: Introduction

Part 2: The facts

Part 3: The present proceedings

Part 4: The nature of the obligation to investigate which arises under articles 2 and 3 of the Convention

---

[12] [2001] EWHC Admin 520; *New Law Online* 301066501.

Part 5: Is it arguable that the treatment of Mr Wright by the Prison Service constituted a breach of article 2 or article 3?

Part 6: Has there been an effective official investigation into Mr Wright's death?

Part 7: The appropriate remedy

Part 8: The claimants' other claims

Part 9: Conclusion

Part 1: Introduction

2. These proceedings concern the death in prison of a young man called Paul Wright. The claimants are his mother and his aunt. The defendant has been variously described as "the Home Office" and "the Secretary of State for the Home Department." At all material times the defendant has acted through the Prison Service.

3. Mr Wright died in prison on 7th November 1996 as a result of a severe asthma attack. Amongst other matters, the claimants contend (i) that the treatment of Mr Wright in the period leading up to his death constituted a breach of articles 2 and 3 of the European Convention on Human Rights ("the Convention"); (ii) that the defendant's failure since 7th November 1996 properly to investigate Mr Wright's death is a continuing breach of the procedural obligation arising under articles 2 and 3 to enquire into possible breaches of those articles..."

ARBITRATION

- Introduction – background to the reference and jurisdiction.

- What are the contentious issues to be decided.

- Outline of the principal facts.

- Findings on the facts and application of the law as appropriate.

- Making of award.

There is a fairly marked difference between writing an arbitrator's award and giving judgment: an award is not expected to condescend to the same level of detail as the approach of a judge. This becomes obvious in connection with setting out the law, which ordinarily would be limited. In an area which is essentially one of private justice, the range of personal style is even greater, although a model General Checklist of the structure of an award is offered to practitioners by the Chartered Institute of Arbitrators. This suggests the following framework:

1.   Heading or Title

1.1 Reference to the relevant Arbitration Act or jurisdiction

1.2 The Parties

1.3. The Title

1.4. Identify the Arbitrator

1.5. Provide an index where applicable

2.   Recitals

2.1. Identify with sufficient particularity the Arbitration Agreement

2.2. The Appointment of the Arbitrator

2.3. Interlocutory matters

2.4. Site Visit, if any

2.5. Evidence, submissions and matters received for consideration

3.   Background

3.1. History of the claim

3.2. Nature of the relief sought

4.   Argument

4.1. Contentions of the Parties

4.2. Findings on the evidence

4.3. Findings on the argument

5.   The Award

5.1. Heading: "For the reasons stated above I therefore now award and direct that…"

5.2. Making of Monetary Award and by when it is to be paid

5.3. Making of Performance Award if applicable and by when performance to be undertaken.

5.4. Interest

5.5. Costs

5.6. Award to be dated and signed by Arbitrator and witnessed.

7.6

WRITING TRIBUNAL DECISIONS

Although the number, variety and specific function of tribunals make it difficult to generalise about the writing of tribunal decisions there are a number of features in common. All decisions and awards are reserved. They are in the form of uniform decisions in writing. They are written by the legally qualified chairman and give the impression of collegiality, although very occasionally the chairman will report the existence of a dissenting opinion within the award. For the purpose of judicial certainty a dissenting view does not affect the outcome, although it may well prompt an appeal.

Invariably tribunal awards have a structure which conforms either to an unspecified but regularly used previous pattern, or to a model suggested in the training of tribunal members or the Appeals Service which tends to be more extensive than that given to recorders and district judges who will previously have been senior legal practitioners. Those who sit on tribunals have a wider variety of background and experience. Some are legally qualified, some are professionally qualified and some are lay people. Like the JSB courses, emphasis in the training of tribunal members is placed upon practical participation. The most successful training courses are often those characterised by a high level of participation in the form of role-play, case studies and discussion groups.

You must recognise that there is a marked difference in the way in which decisions are prepared in different tribunals. This is less surprising if you consider that while the majority of tribunals deal with the adversarial system in much the same way as our courts, some, such as the Transport Tribunal, tackle appeals from an inquisitorial process. These are rarely adversarial and generally conform to a template, although even if their structure is individual, the approach of any particular tribunal in producing succinct reasons for decisions may provide lessons for all.

At the lowest level the tribunal determines legal liability by way of adjudication in respect of what may be an administrative process or function of local government. A good example is that of the Parking Adjudicator.[13] A person

---

[13] See *Decision Drafting: Brief, Balanced and to the Point* Martin Wood (2001) 8 *Tribunals Journal* 2.

wishing to challenge the issue of fixed penalty parking notice has a statutory right of appeal. The parties may choose for appeals to be dealt with either at a personal hearing or as a postal case. Adjudicators sit alone. Normally they take cases from a general list and will not have seen the case beforehand. Personal hearings are informal. Generally only the appellant attends. Parties are rarely legally represented. The adjudicator and the appellant view the imaged documents on the computer and the adjudicator hears the appellant's oral evidence and representations. The adjudicator normally gives the decision immediately and keys it into a computer with a template for the decision ready. When the adjudicator closes the case, the decision notice is automatically printed for the appellant to take away. The decision in postal cases is automatically generated overnight and dispatched next day. There are currently about 40,000 appeals annually.

With such a workload, the time to devote to preparing and delivering a decision is at a premium. Even apart from the demands such a concentration of appeals brings, parking contraventions are minor matters and the time devoted to them should be proportionate. On the other hand, they do concern the local authority imposing a penalty on the citizen. Parking enforcement can be a highly emotive subject and appellants frequently feel deeply aggrieved. The need for expedition must be balanced against ensuring that the appellant feels that, if he loses, he has had a fair opportunity to put his case and received a fair trial.

Consider then that Employment Tribunals are dealing with people's livelihoods; that Immigration Tribunals, particularly those dealing in asylum claims, may literally be concerned with matters of life and death, working under the spotlight of a hostile media. If care is needed for a Parking Adjudicator, working under immense pressure, in assuaging anger over what is really a minor matter, how very important it is for those constructing tribunal awards dealing with issues that have a considerable impact on the lives of those before them to ensure that the decision and the reasons for it are clear and readily understood.

For the Parking Adjudicator the skill is to produce as brief a decision as quickly as possible while satisfying the principle of giving adequate reasons that are intelligible and deal with the substantive points raised. While this is perhaps no different as a standard from decision-writing by tribunals in general, brevity is fostered by the technical constraints of the computer system used for this particular scheme, which allows a maximum of 1,500 characters to be entered in the 'reasons box'. This equates to roughly 250 words.

On any view the adjudicator must use language economically and put his reasons into plain English. The limitations of space therefore promote a highly disciplined approach to decision-writing. This affects the entire decision-making process since adjudicators must be rigorous, even ruthless, in identifying the essential issues and discarding irrelevancies. Moreover, since there are a number of situations which arise over and again, reasoning in such cases can be reduced to a regular form of words which can be cut and pasted into the pro forma decision document as appropriate.

This may appear to be a harsh and fairly arbitrary form of justice, appropriate to a first-level only tribunal, but it suits the working regime of this particular jurisdiction. In terms of a broader direction to tribunals, it is not out of step with the House of Lords view on tribunal awards:

> "[Reasons] need not be elaborate nor lengthy. But they should be such as to tell the parties in broad terms why the decision was reached. In many cases ... a very few sentences should suffice to give such explanation as is appropriate to the particular situation."[14]

---

[14] *Stefan* v *General Medical Council* [1999] 1 WLR 1293 per Lord Clyde @ 1303G *et seq.*

7.7

A GENERAL APPROACH

Application of the Human Rights Act 1998 ensures that in fact all of the essential elements are contained in a written tribunal decision:

- summary of the issues;

- relevant findings of fact;

- the reasons why the decision follows from the facts.

The JSB and Tribunals and Appeals Service provide training to both lay members and legal chairmen in drafting the more extensive reasons needed either to meet the request of a party or by statute. Guidance is also given by both second-tier appellate tribunals, particularly in the employment and immigration fields, and by the Court of Appeal. This can be reduced to the following broad areas.

IDENTIFY THE ISSUES

Tribunals frequently have to deal with unrepresented parties. This can lead to the failure of Originating Applications disclosing either the appropriate or indeed any cause of action. Both the parties and the tribunal should know precisely what issues arise for determination at the hearing, and therefore what is required of the decision or award. Many cases involve multiple complaints, which require the assessment of both sequential and overlapping issues, the determination of which might give completely different remedies in law or none at all, depending on the findings of fact.

FINDING THE FACTS

While it is not necessary to recite the entirety of the evidence it is necessary to make findings in respect of all facts material to the outcome of the tribunal's conclusion. A failure to do so may amount to an error in law allowing an appeal. It is not necessary to decide every disputed question of fact, however tangential, but material facts in issue must be decided.

TELLING THE TALE

The easiest way in which to structure a written decision, and the most effective, is to provide an orderly sequence of the key events relevant to the dispute. This should incorporate non-contentious items which can be drawn from a prepared chronology, as well as those found by the tribunal. It is good practice, in telling the parties why they have won or lost, to explain the thought process that has led the tribunal to prefer the evidence of one side to the other on particular issues.[15] It is not unusual that for some issues the evidence of one side may be preferred, on other issues, that of the opposing side.

SETTING OUT THE LAW

All tribunals are creatures of statute. Invariably their practice and procedure and the substantive remedies for which tribunals are employed are set out in delegated legislation, either domestic or European. It is good practice to set out the relevant statutory provisions considered by the tribunal in order to reflect their relevant jurisdiction, together with any relevant guidance notes or directions issued on the subject. It is not necessary to refer to authority as precedent, since the principles of law will be applied to the facts as found in each case.

THE PARTIES' SUBMISSIONS

It is helpful for the first level tribunal or the first appellate level tribunal to summarise the rival contentions of the parties in argument, not least so that on appeal or further appeal it can be seen what points were or were not taken below, particularly where rules restrict new points being taken for the first time on appeal. It is also desirable that the parties see from the tribunal's reasons that all of their appropriate arguments were considered and why they were accepted or rejected: the parties are entitled to be told why they have won or lost.[16]

STATING THE CONCLUSIONS

Having set out the issues, the findings of fact, the law and the parties' submissions, the critical task for the tribunal is to offer a conclusion which discloses a logical process of reasoning which leads to a permissible conclusion. If the tribunal is confident and logical in its reasoning, and has addressed all of the

---

[15] See also *Telling them Why they've Won or Lost* HH Judge Peter Clark (2001) 8 *Tribunals Journal* 11.
[16] *Meek v Birmingham District Council* [1987] IRLR 250.

material issues, an appeal will lie only on a point of law unless there is no evidence to support a finding of fact. Clear and pertinent conclusions reduce substantially the risk of a decision being set aside for the inadequacy of an explanation.

MAJORITY DECISIONS

The decision-making process of the tribunal involves active discussion between the members of the panel to come to agreement over the various issues and the outcome. Lay members are likely to take advice on the law from the chairman. It may happen that members of the tribunal cannot agree on the result, and even occasions where the chairman, upon whom the obligation to write the tribunal reasons rests, is in the minority. He should not permit members who dissent to write their own dissenting judgment. The expertise is his, and even if he disagrees with his colleagues, it is his duty to ensure that their views are properly expressed in the decision.

INTERLOCUTORY RULINGS AND ORDERS

In view of the application of Article 6.1 ECHR, where a ruling on procedural matters is required, either during the hearing or on an interlocutory basis, a written decision together with short reasons for the ruling should be given. This may cover applications to amend, the admissibility of evidence, the question of witness orders, disclosure directions, or applications for an adjournment. This follows the general practice, following a directions hearing, of the chairman setting out the orders made on that occasion, with short reasons showing why disputed issues were decided as they were.

7.8

MODEL DECISION WRITING

Beyond training exercises, certain appellate tribunals commend particular decisions as models of their kind at first instance level. One such was the Employment Tribunal decision of *Deman* v *Association of University Teachers and others*[17] which featured complaints of race discrimination and victimisation, and was commended by the Employment Appeals Tribunal as a model of its kind. The structure of the decision is therefore worthy of analysis:

1. Decision: the outcome, both as to the complaints and the claim for costs.

2. Extended Reasons:
2.1. History: placing the present complaints in context.
2.2. History of these proceedings – preliminary hearings and directions concerning pleadings, disclosure, exchange of witness statements, further information.
2.3. Conduct of this hearing: rulings given by the tribunal during the course of the hearing, with short reasons for the decision.
2.4. Issues: recording the tribunal's understanding of what the issues are in the matter.
2.5. The evidence:
   i   An outline of the evidence received, both oral and documentary.
   ii Findings of fact made in relation to the evidence in respect of each issue, together with reasons for the findings made.
   iii General findings of fact.
2.6. Relevant legislation: each statute and each relevant section.
2.7. The legal test to be applied.
2.8. The burden of proof.
2.9. Application of the legal test and burden of proof to the facts as found in respect of each issue.

3. Overall conclusion.

4. Costs, and reasons for costs awards.

---

[17] 12 November, 2002 Case Nos.6004846/99 and 220101/99.

7.9
WRITING APPELLATE JUDGMENTS

It is difficult to apply a formulaic approach to writing judgments on appeals since the constitution of appeal courts allows not only for collegial and individual judgments but also the expression of dissenting opinion. Other than the designated lead judgment writer, each judge is free to contribute as much or as little as he wishes. It is important however, to have set out in the overall scheme of as many judgments as are being delivered the appropriate components. These are essentially:

- The primary facts.

- The decision below.

- Issues on the appeal.

- The law and or test to be applied.

- Application of the test and law to the facts as found.

In appeals at the lowest level, particularly matters of procedure dealt with summarily, and therefore an examination of rulings of the District Judge or Master, matters can be taken shortly. The case need only be outlined very briefly; there is no need for the facts except those relevant to the appeal. There is always a short cut to the decision-making process, namely that the tribunal below was not demonstrably wrong. Often the court is able to say there that the true ambit of the appeal is the exercise of a discretion, and although a different tribunal may have exercised it differently, there is nothing inherently wrong with the exercise of the discretion in question. Beyond that, opposing submissions should fall within a relatively narrow compass for assessment by the appellate judge.

7.10

APPELLATE TRIBUNAL AWARDS

The composition and structure of appellate tribunals are so diverse and their statutory jurisdiction so varied that it is difficult to deal generically with appellate tribunal decision drafting. It is not within the scope of this work to examine the approach of specific statutory bodies within the burgeoning appellate tribunals sector.[18] However it is worth noting that the system of tiered appellate tribunals produces a substantial body of case records, and in some areas of law these take the form of binding or persuasive authority.

An example of an intermediate or first level appellate tribunal is the generically named Appeals Tribunals Service, which was launched in 2000 to arrange and hear appeals on decisions on:

- Social Security

- Child Support

- Housing Benefit

- Council Tax Benefit

- Vaccine Damage

- Tax Credit

- Compensation Recovery

- Child Tax Credit

- Pensions Credit

---

[18] For further information see Civil Appeals, EMS 2004 and *www.tribunals-review.org.uk* in respect of such appeals bodies as the General and Special Commissioners of Income Tax; VAT and Duties Tribunal; Transport Tribunal; Pensions Appeal Tribunal; Lands Tribunal; Independent Schools Tribunal; Special Immigration Appeals Commission; Consumer Credit Licensing Appeals Tribunal; Estate Agent Appeals Tribunal; Competition Commission Appeals Tribunal; Wireless Telegraphy Appeals Tribunal; Parking Appeals Service; Family Health Service Appeals Authority; NHS Medicines (Control of Prices and Profits) Appeal Tribunal; Reserve Forces Appeal Tribunal; Department of Education Exclusion Appeals Panel and Admission Appeals Panel; Registered Nursery Inspectors' Appeals Tribunal; and the Criminal Injuries Compensation Appeals Tribunal.

The nomenclature is equally confusing as to the level of jurisdiction: for example the Transport Tribunal, comprised of a legally-qualified chairman and lay members, hears appeals from the Traffic Commissioners; however decisions of the Appeals Tribunal are appealed to the single Social Security and Child Support Commissioner. For our purposes it is important to note first, that certain tiers of tribunal such as the Office of the Social Security and Child Support Commissioners were established as specialist appellate bodies in order to make case law, and second that such bodies as the Employment Appeals Tribunal and the Immigration Appeals Tribunal are superior courts of record in their own right providing authoritative guidance to tribunals and practitioners.

As with most judgment writing, the appellate tribunal drafting its decision faces a variety of audiences though much depends on the tier of appeal as will be apparent from the foregoing. It must be conscious not only of addressing the parties, but how the decision may be used as a binding or persuasive authority in the future. The readership will include not only lawyers but also other professional or expert advisers, other tribunals, writers of textbooks and commentaries, and potentially, the next level of appellate tribunal or the Court of Appeal. Cases that will be restricted to the immediacy of the parties may be dealt with briefly, setting out the facts, the decision and brief reasons. Some cases are destined for the close attention of a wide readership,[19] particularly if dealing with a highly focused area of the law, or the interpretation of the appropriate regulations. This type of decision requires:

- a reasonably comprehensive assessment of the law;

- a reproduction of the appropriate legislation;

- a history of the claim;

- a history of the appeal process;

- the arguments of the parties;

- any relevant arguments not advanced by the parties;

- the decision;

- reasons for the decision.

Subject to the real problem of not being able to generalise adequately, there are a number of distinct categories that appellate tribunals look for in deciding whether they are able to interfere with a first instance decision. These are:

---

[19] See Howard Levinson *The Written Decisions of Social Security Commissioners* (2000) 7 *Tribunals Journal* 16.

i   where the decision appears on its face to contain a false proposition of law;

ii   where the decision is unsupported by evidence;

iii   where the decision is founded on irrelevant evidence;

iv   where no reasonable tribunal could have arrived at that decision on the facts as found or agreed;

v   where there has been a sufficient breach of procedural requirements to impeach the decision under the Human Rights Act 1998 or the rules of natural justice;

vi   where the reasons for the decision were inadequate in form;

vii   where the reasons for the decision were inadequate in content.

The decision will usually be drafted around any of these relevant core propositions. Any error of law must be identified, and the arguments advanced by the parties, or by the appellate tribunal itself, considered, analysed and disposed of.

7.11
COURT OF APPEAL JUDGMENTS

Court of Appeal judgments are intended for relatively sophisticated audiences and are directed at the legal teams rather than litigants themselves, unless appearing in person. They are nearly always reported (electronically if not in hard copy) and it is therefore of the utmost importance that they be clear not only to lawyers but also to other judges who will have to read and apply them. There must be no doubt as to what was decided and, equally importantly for the purpose of precedent or guidance, what was not.

The judgments in most Court of Appeal Civil Division appeals are reserved, or at least considered over an adjournment. The danger of proceeding to give an *ex tempore* judgment at this level is changing the decision as one goes along. For those judgments that are delivered *ex tempore* the judges will in fact be prepared beforehand, since they are able to take the facts and substance of the legal argument from counsel's skeleton arguments, chronology and written submissions, and, for permission hearings, any précis provided by judicial assistants. The process is usually one of making the decision, even on occasion indicating what the outcome is, and afterwards writing a judgment to justify it.

An exception to this approach concerns applications for permission to appeal. Here judgments are almost always *ex tempore* and invariably a different audience is being addressed. This is the occasion on which a clear explanation of a refusal to give permission must be given directly to the litigant – he must understand why this is the end of the road for his claim – and sufficient reasons included to enable him to accept that proper thought has been given to his problem. Despite Article 6 Convention rights, my research indicates that there are still occasions when permission is refused without any or any adequate reasons being given.

PART 8
USING LAW REPORTS: FUNDAMENTALS AND DIFFICULTIES

8

USING LAW REPORTS: FUNDAMENTALS AND DIFFICULTIES

The doctrine of *stare decisis* and the order of precedent mean that judgments of the superior courts are primary sources of law. It should not take a whole section of this book to remind you, when reading a law report, it is only the judgment which constitutes the source material, yet the point is so important and so often overlooked that it requires more than a line or two. The headnote is no part of the judgment: it is merely an editorial summary of the facts, the decision and the reasoning, and is an innovation thought to have commenced in *Burrow's Reports* c. 1765. Likewise any legal taxonomy provided to assist with searching for authorities in the same area is only editorial guidance.

The law reporter performs three useful functions. He selects judgments of sufficient importance to publish; he categorises them; and he analyses judgments by producing a headnote summary, so that, on the face of it, you do not have to. This results in considerable convenience and time saving, particularly if the series of reports are readily searchable or have a half-decent index.

To that extent law reports should be regarded as aided discovery – they are edited to draw the attention of the reader to vital passages. In certain series of reports editorial policy takes this function literally. In *Lloyds' Law Reports* (extended to all LLP reports) key passages in the judgments are marked with a bold marginal line. This is a useful feature when you are presented with such an authority at the last minute, and consistent too with the Practice Directions[1] on citing, identifying and or marking up the passages of judgments relied upon in argument, which judges are encouraged to pre-read. Editorial markings are intended to be instructive but are in fact matters of opinion. In the final analysis you must analyse the judgment yourself.

---

[1] *Practice Direction (Judgments: Form and Citation)* [2001] 1 WLR 194 para 2.5; *Practice Direction (Court of Appeal: Citation of Authorities)* [2001] 1 WLR 1001; CPR Part 52 PD (30th June 2004) para 15.11(2)(a); and see *Scribes West Ltd v Relsa Anstalt* (No 1) [2004] EWCA (Civ) 835 per Brooke LJ.

Reading law reports to support or undermine argument is the most common process of syntopical reading (see Part 3.5) in which lawyers engage. However even the most instructive of opinions that form the headnote of a report has editorial limitations due to the need for condensation. As a matter of course you should always question the authority and accuracy of the headnote, since any reliance upon headnotes for convenience should be made sparingly. They may be wrong. They may not be exhaustive. You may be able to discover important meanings that the editor of the commentary has not discovered or has consciously suppressed as being subsidiary to the main thrust of the case.

8.1

THE FUNCTIONALITY OF LAW REPORTS

Lawyers who come to read law reports usually have one of two aims in mind. They are either searching for support for a legal proposition: the support they seek may be positive or negative; it may be directly on the point or tangential; it may be a fair comparable, *a fortiori* or an illustration of *reductio in absurdum*; it may, in fact, not exist. Or second, practitioners will have been alerted to a specific authority, which they need to assess to decide whether it will support their position or impair that of their opponent.

For those searching for authority they:

- Need to have some idea of what they want to know;

- Must have at least some idea of where to find out what they want to know;

- Must know what kind of questions they are asking and in which kinds of law reports the material can be found;

- Must know how the particular work is organised.

Those reading an identified authority should:

- Read the substantive judgments before the headnote;

- Failing that, they should identify the leading majority judgment and read that before reading the headnote;

- Form a view of the *ratio* or *rationes decidendi* before reading the headnote;

- *Not* read a commentary before reading at least the leading judgment.

Refusing the temptation to read the headnote or commentary first in order to save time is a difficult discipline to master in practice. However it follows one of the rules of intrinsic reading:[2] you should read an author's preface and

---

[2] Adler *op. cit.* p. 174.

introduction before reading his book, but should not read a commentary until afterwards. This is because it may distort your reading as you will see only the points identified by the commentator and have no unclouded view of your own, free of another's influence. The law reporter who edits a headnote for your convenience is no less a commentator on the judgment he is analysing for you, since he forms his own view of what is important enough to distil and, particularly, what he regards to be the *ratio*. Moreover some series of specialist law reports have a commentary which precedes the report: see, for example, *Housing Law Reports* or *Industrial Relations Law Reports*.

Your view of the worth of a formal commentary may be conditioned by the respect in which a particular editor is held, or any previous experience that you found particularly helpful or unhelpful. But it should never be used as a substitute for forming your own views about the particular worth of an authority or its relevance to the legal problem with which you are engaged. Equally if you rely on a digest or the headnote of a case, a partial picture may lead to a mistaken view of the whole. This is evident from citation references in textbooks and practice books where either the full judgments of cases cited do not actually convey support for the proposition advanced, or the editing creates an impression not borne out by a close inspection of the judgments.[3]

---

[3] See, for example the commentary on *Walkley* v *Precision Forgings Ltd* [1979] 1 WLR 606 and *Whitfield* v *North Durham Health Authority*[1995] 6 Med. L.R. 32 CA at 8–70 vol 2 Civil Procedure 2004 *('The White Book'* p.2075).

8.2

ACCURACY IN LAW REPORTING

The practitioner should have two particular concerns with the accuracy of law reporting. First, the accuracy with which judgments are recorded and reproduced; second, the reliability of the editorial opinion expressed in the headnote.

The precision with which early law reporting was conducted is highly questionable. In the absence of the court rolls you are properly entitled to consider whether, before 1865, any reported judgments under consideration were in fact themselves subject to editorial opinion. Many important cases dating up to the mid-nineteenth century contain judgments which are extremely short, and are fairly obviously *a précis* based solely on the reporter's note.[4] Until the nineteenth century printed books were still an expensive commodity and the space available for individual reports was limited: the older the authority prior to the seventeenth century, the more expensive it would have been to produce. No wonder law reporters were either encouraged to be brief, or, if they were privately printing their own reports, it paid them to be so.

The system of freelance law reporting was haphazard at best, and at worst dangerously anecdotal. It is certainly apparent that judgments were neither handed down in written form nor dictated for the benefit of the law reporters present. The contents and subject matter varied between the many hundreds of reports named after the reporter or occasionally after particular judges,[5] and subsequently collected together and published as the English Reports (1900–1932). These and others, which form the huge body of Nominate Reports, were roundly criticised by 1863 as enormously expensive, prolix, irregular in publication and delayed.[6]

---

[4] See, for example *Atkyn's Chancery Reports* 3 vols. 1737–1754; *Holt's Kings Bench Reports* 1688–1710.

[5] *Atkyn's Reports* were named after Baron Cursitor of the Court of Exchequer (1736–1755) and are described as reports from the High Court of Chancery under the Chancellorship of Lord Hardwicke; *Holt's Reports* were compiled from a manuscript of Thomas Farresley, a barrister of Middle Temple, who kept a record of all cases determined by Sir John Holt, LCJ (1688–1710).

[6] See reference to the letter of WTS Daniel QC to Sir Roundell Palmer S-G referred to in The Incorporated Council's *135 Years of Law Reporting for England and Wales* Paul Magrath (ICLR Sept 2001).

Beyond that the reliability of many reporters was questionable. Key facts that it was essential for the reader to know were often missed out.[7] Some series were notoriously bad, for example Barnardiston (*Reports in Chancery 1726–35; King's Bench Reports 1726–35*), Espinasse (six volumes between 1793 and 1807) and the *Modern Reports* (1669–1732) and on a number of occasions judges declined to receive citation from counsel of their reports.[8] The accuracy and substance of Kelyng (*Pleas of the Crown 1789*) has also been much argued over.[9] By relatively modern times courts were prepared to be openly sceptical of the value of early reports.[10]

You may rightly be concerned about the frequency with which Nominate Reports are still cited today. As long ago as 1925 there was a movement to discard the use of many of the older reports and decisions. Carleton Kemp Allen wrote in the *Law Quarterly Review* "We have more to fear from an exaggerated respect for antiquity than from innovating judges."[11]

In 1849 a report of the Law Amendment Society observed that "even if all the reports which are published are correct and given by competent persons, they are now so numerous that they cannot be known to one tithe of the practitioners of the law. They are beyond the reach not only of the public, but of the great body of the profession." To move the process forward Nathaniel Lindley QC, afterwards Master of the Rolls and a Law Lord, produced a paper in 1863 in which he set out the objectives of a law report and the criteria for the selection of cases.

To be included a case should:

- introduce, or appear to introduce, a new principle or a new rule;
- materially modify an existing principle or rule;
- settle, or materially tend to settle, a question on which the law is doubtful;
- be for any reason peculiarly instructive.

Lindley also gave guidance on what should not be reported:

[7] See for example *Williams v Carwardine* (1833) 4 B & A 621 which omits to tell the reader whether the plaintiff was aware that a reward had been offered for information; in *Fouldes v Willoughby* (1841) 8 M & W 549 several important facts are missing. Yet both of these cases were regarded as leading authorities for many years.
[8] See *Slater v May* (1704) 2 Ld. Raym. 1071; 92 ER 210; *Small v Nairne* (1849) 13 QB @ 844; 116 ER @ 1486.
[9] *Woolmington v DPP* [1935] AC 462, per Lord Sankey LC @ 479.
[10] See *In Re Canadian Oil Works Corporation* (1875) LR 10 CH 593 per James LJ @ 600; *Moore v Landauer* [1921] 2 KB 519 per Bankes LJ @532.
[11] (1925) 163 LQR 342.

- cases which pass without discussion or consideration, and are therefore valueless as a precedent;

- cases which are substantially repetitions of what is reported already.

In November, 1864 the Bar adopted a scheme to publish the decisions of the superior courts of law and equity under the management of a Council composed of members of the Inns of Court and the Incorporated Law Society, in accordance with the Lindley criteria, and to ensure accuracy of reporting, uniformity of appearance, and breadth of coverage. The Council of Law Reporting was duly established and its first reports were published in November 1865. These have since been regarded as "The Law Reports", an official, authorised series which takes priority in the order of citation over every other type of law report in which the same case may be found.[12]

In 1891 the Council introduced the dated annual volumes in the four series currently entitled *Appeal Cases, Chancery, Queen's Bench* and *Family Reports*. Between 1866 and 1953 the Council also published *Weekly Notes* which covered additional cases that did not merit an appearance in the Law Reports, and made case summaries available more quickly. *Weekly Law Reports* superseded this publication in 1953 where the full length law reports in volumes 2 and 3 were produced much faster than their subsequent appearance in the Law Reports, and those in volume 1 did not afterwards appear there. Subsequently the Council produced *Industrial Cases Reports* in 1972 with the opening of the short-lived National Industrial Relations Court by the Heath government.

The authoritative voice of these reports comes from their having been proof read by the judges and counsel involved in the case, and by the inclusion of counsel's argument in a form approved by counsel themselves. This delays publication but that is made up for by the accuracy of reporting. Ever since the inclusion of cases in the Law Reports, 'Weeklies' or 'ICR' has been guided by Lord Lindley's principles. Hopefully most other commercially available reports are.

Editorial opinion as to whether or not a case should be reported is also influenced by whether a judgment is considered important at the time when it is delivered. Sometimes cases which went unreported are cited to good effect, and are reported subsequent to the case in which they were used.[13] In *Grand Metropolitan Nominee (No.2) Co. Ltd.* v *Evans*, heard in the Court of Appeal in March 1992, the case of *Re Jokai Tea Trading,* which had been heard in 1989,

---

[12] See *Practice Direction(Judgments: Form and Citation)* [2001] 1 WLR 194 and *Bank of Scotland* v *Butcher, The Times* 13.02.03 (see also Part 3.10 on the use of precedents).
[13] See for example *Mesher* v *Mesher and Hall (Note)* [1980] 1 All ER 126;

was cited and applied. When *Grand Metropolitan* was reported at [1992] 1 WLR 1191, *Jokai Tea* was reported as a Practice Note immediately afterwards at [1992] 1 WLR 1196.

While the doctrine of *stare decisis* and the use of precedents make the accuracy of law reporting of immense importance, this pressure is also balanced with a need for speed – to get the law out to practitioners and judges. The need for decisions being reported early led to the success of Butterworth's *All England Law Reports* from 1936, popular both for its swiftness of reporting and breadth of coverage. The law does not stand still for a day, and counsel who fail to notice a relevant new authority in *The Times* on the day of the trial, or check with an electronic daily alerter or *Casetrack* will be doing their clients and the judge no favour.

The last twenty years has gradually seen the introduction of more and more specialised commercially produced law reports, to such an extent that it seems there are now almost as many titles available as the period prior to 1865. This often leads to the suggestion that there is too much law! Many practitioners' journals such as the *Solicitors Journal, Justice of the Peace* and *New Law Journal* have always regularly produced law reports; some, for example *Estates Gazette* and *Construction Law Journal* have developed a series of their law reports which stand independently from the parent journal itself, as has the London *Times*. But highly specialised law reports with editors drawn from practice in the areas of professional negligence, building, family law, patent cases, company law, immigration, and many others have emerged to provide the lawyer with as much choice as his counterpart of 150 years ago, and the judges are now concerned by this proliferation. The Court of Appeal has now directed[14] that a bundle of authorities filed on an appeal should in general not contain more than ten authorities unless the scale of the appeal warrants more extensive citation; failure to comply may have adverse costs consequences.

Occasionally in the past judges used the Law Reports as an opportunity to make slight editorial corrections. Lord Denning in particular was not averse to modifying his judgments, the most well-known example being in *Ghani* v *Jones*.[15] In the original oral judgment Lord Denning MR apparently said, "The police officers must have reasonable grounds to believe that the person in possession of the property has himself committed the crime or is implicated in it or is accessory to it." As reported the words "or at any rate his refusal must be quite unreasonable" were added, substantially altering the conclusion, and making a qualification the practical effect of which was to enable police to take away property from a person who was innocent of the crime. The editors

---

[14] By CPR Part 52 PD para 15.11(2)(c) effective 30th June 2004.
[15] [1970] 1 QB 693; [1969] 3 All ER 1700;[1969] 3 WLR 1158. See the discussion *Law Reporting and the Amending Hand* (1970) NLJ 423.

of the *Law Quarterly Review* identified[16] it as the most striking instance of altering a judgment before it appeared in its final form since *National Sailor's and Fireman's Union* v *Reed*[17] where Mr Justice Astbury amended the grounds on which he had held the General Strike of 1926 to be illegal so as to ensure that his decision concerning the illegality of the strike was not considered as *obiter dictum*. The journal made the point that Sir Frederick Pollock, then the editor of the *Law Reports*, did not draw attention to the change in any editorial note.

In the age of electronic reporting full copies of judgments to be posted as reports will not appear until they have been approved by the judge concerned within 28 days of a digest appearing. Amendments may occur, but anything other than minor spelling, grammatical or syntactical changes will be discussed with counsel before publication. Occasionally substantive revisions are made and revised judgments handed down for publication.[18]

Substantive conflict between facts contained in reports of the same case published in different titles is rare, but does happen. An example occurred in the judgment of Lord Justice Evershed in *Davies* v *Swan Motor Co. (Swansea) Ltd* which was reported in both [1949] 2 KB 291 @ 319 and [1949] 1 All ER 620 @ 629. The curious feature here is that the words reportedly used in the transcript of Lord Justice Evershed's judgment are different. Here is the Law Reports' version at p. 319 with the differences contained in the All England version at p.629 added in bold type. Words in the Law Report omitted from the All England report appear italicised and in brackets:

"Therefore, his position in relation to other road users must in part at least at any particular point of time depend upon what the driver of his own vehicle did. When all the facts are examined (and anticipating somewhat the answer to the third question) it will be seen that the two drivers (the omnibus driver and the lorry driver) were so incautious in their performances that their two vehicles were involved in a collision. On the facts of the case it seems to me to be [*quite*] plain that no doctrine of "last opportunity," if such there is or was, could be applied. One could not fairly say of anybody here that they had a "last opportunity" [*for*] **of** avoiding the accident and in fact in the general mêlée which resulted, the deceased suffered, and suffered most grievously, partly as the result of the hazardous position which he occupied in relation to the two vehicles.

---

[16] See Notes (1970) 86 LQR 299.
[17] [1926] 1 Ch 536; see also (1926) 42 LQR 289,290.
[18] See *Moy* v *Pettman Smith* reported as [2002] PNLR 961 CA with a modified supplementary judgment reported as *Moy* v *Pettman Smith (No 2)(Note)* at [2003] EWCA Civ 466; [2003] PNLR 606.

Looked at in that way, this case seems to me to be different on its facts from such a case as would have arisen if the lorry had proceeded straight along the road, and the omnibus had tried to pass it without there being sufficient room for it so to do. With all respect to the learned judge in the court below, I have therefore come to the conclusion that his finding that there was no contributory negligence within the meaning of the Act of 1945 cannot stand, and that on the facts the fair common-sense view to take of the matter is that which has been proposed by my Lord. I only add this[, if I may]. I express the hope that there [*should be and*] will be no divergence of principle or of the application of principle between the Admiralty Courts and the Common Law Courts, in dealing with [*these*] matters of contributory negligence under the **Maritime Conventions Act, 1911 and the Law Reform (Married Women and Tortfeasors) Act 1935** [Acts of 1911 and 1945] respectively. [*It seems to me that, broadly regarded,*] **In substance** the intention of the two Acts [was, in substance,] the same, so that similar principles should apply and be applied in the same way.

It only remains for me to add a few words in regard to the third question: Can the omnibus company require the driver of the lorry, James, to contribute to the damage which in the action the omnibus company must pay, namely, four-fifths of the figure awarded by the learned judge? Again, with all respect to the learned judge, I cannot see that the answers which he accepted to that claim are made out. It seems to me that on the facts, particularly the outstanding fact [*as found*] that the lorry driver, James, started to turn across the main road without giving any warning signal in time, it is impossible to resist the conclusion that James also caused, in part, the accident by his negligence, and, taking that view, I see no reason to differ from the apportionment of blame which Cassels J. thought appropriate, namely, two-thirds to the omnibus driver and one-third to the lorry driver. [*As I indicated, there remains under this head the question whether the relationship between James and the deceased was such that if the deceased were suing James, the contributory negligence point would produce arithmetically some different result from that which we have indicated should apply as between the deceased and the omnibus company. I do not think there is any ground for supposing that there is, or ought to be, arithmetically, any difference.*]"

8.3
EDITORIAL ANOMALIES

What is far less rare is the difference of editorial style or opinion that creeps into the headnotes of reports of the same case reported in different series. Two examples are sufficient to prove the point. First, in *Bell v Peter Browne & Co*[19] the Law Reports provide the following catchwords for the Court of Appeal decision:

"Limitation of Action – Contract, breach of – Negligence – Transfer of matrimonial home by plaintiff to wife subject to interest in proceeds of sale – Solicitors failing to protect plaintiff's interest in proceeds of sale – Solicitors' failure continuing to be remediable so long as matrimonial home unsold – Wife selling matrimonial home after six years had elapsed and spending entire proceeds – Plaintiff claiming damages against solicitors for professional negligence – Whether claim statute-barred"

The All England Law Reports[20] have the following catchwords for the same case:

"Solicitor – Negligence – Cause of action – Parallel claims in tort and contract- Limitation of action – Accrual of cause of action – Divorce – Matrimonial home in joint names of husband and wife – Property trans-ferred into sole name of wife under agreement entitling husband to share of proceeds on sale – Solicitors failing to prepare declaration of trust or mortgage or register caution to protect husband's interest – wife selling property eight years later and spending proceeds –Husband losing share in proceeds of sale and suing solicitors – When cause of action against solic-itors accruing in contract and tort – Whether husband's cause of action time-barred."

The *Law Reports* provide the following headnote:

"In October 1977, following the breakdown of his marriage, the plaintiff consulted the defendants, a firm of solicitors. He discussed

---

[19] [1990] 2 QB 495.
[20] [1990] 3 All ER 124.

with them what was to happen to the matrimonial home, which was registered in the joint names of the plaintiff and his wife. The plaintiff agreed that the house would be transferred into the sole name of his wife, that it should not then be sold but that he would receive one-sixth of the gross proceeds of sale whenever that sale occurred. His continuing interest in the house would be protected by a trust deed or a mortgage. On 1 September 1978 the plaintiff executed a transfer of the house into his wife's sole name but the defendants took no steps to protect his one-sixth share in the proceeds of sale; no declaration of trust or mortgage was prepared or executed. The plaintiff and his wife were divorced during 1979. In December 1986 the plaintiff was told by his former wife that she had sold the former matrimonial home and had spent all the proceeds, thereby depriving the plaintiff of his one-sixth interest in the proceeds of the sale. The plaintiff issued a writ in August 1987 against the defendants claiming damages for professional negligence. The defendants issued a summons to strike out the plaintiff's statement of claim on the ground that any cause of action was statute-barred. The registrar struck out the plaintiff's action and Auld J. dismissed the plaintiff's appeal.

On appeal by the plaintiff: –

Held, dismissing the appeal, (1) that the failure by the defendants to prepare or execute a formal declaration of trust or other suitable instrument or to cause appropriate entries to be made on the register at the time the property was transferred constituted a breach of contract; that although the defendants' obligations were not discharged by the breach, which remained remediable by lodging a caution until the plaintiff's former wife sold the house, the limitation period began to run from the date of the breach in September 1978, and expired before the issue of the writ in August 1987; and that, accordingly, the claim based on breach of contract was statute-barred (post, pp. *500C, H, 509D-G, 511C-D, 513A-B*). *Midland Bank Trust Co. Ltd. v. Hett, Stubbs & Kemp* [1979] Ch. 384 distinguished.

(2) That a cause of action in negligence did not accrue until damage was suffered; that the plaintiff sustained damage when the transfer was executed and the title to the house passed to the plaintiff's former wife without any formal agreement or protection of the plaintiff's interest in the house or its proceeds of sale, notwithstanding that the defendants' failure to protect the plaintiff's interest by registration remained remediable so long as the house continued to belong to his former wife, and his actual loss remained nominal until the sale by her; and that, accordingly, the claim in negligence against the defendants was also statute-barred (post, pp. *501H – 502B, 503A-D, G*

– 504A, 510E-G, 511C-D). Forster v Outred & Co. [1982] 1 W.L.R. 86,
C.A. and *D. W. Moore & Co. Ltd.* v *Ferrier* [1988] 1 W.L.R. 267, C.A.
applied.

Decision of Auld J. affirmed."

The *All England Reports* provide the following headnote:

"The plaintiff employed the defendant solicitors to act on his behalf
in divorce proceedings when his marriage broke down. The plaintiff
and his wife agreed that the matrimonial home, which was in their
joint names, be transferred into the sole name of the wife, who was to
be entitled to live in it for the time being, and that the plaintiff's
interest in it, which was agreed to be one-sixth of the proceeds of sale,
be protected by a trust deed or mortgage. The house was duly transferred to the wife but the defendants neglected to take any steps to
protect the plaintiff's interest either by arranging for a declaration of
trust or a mortgage to be prepared or by registering a caution in the
Land Registry. Eight years later the wife sold the property and spent
the proceeds. The plaintiff brought an action against the defendants
claiming damages for breach of contract and negligence. The defendants applied to have the action struck out on the ground that it was
time-barred. The registrar granted the application and his decision
was upheld on appeal. The plaintiff appealed.

Held – Where a solicitor negligently fails to take precautions, such as
the registration of a caution or a charge, to protect his client's equitable interest in the proceeds of sale of a property in the sole name of
another party who had agreed that the proceeds would be shared, the
client's cause of action against the solicitor arose in contract when the
breach of duty occurred and in tort when the client parted with his
legal interest in return for an equitable interest or at the latest when a
careful solicitor would have registered a caution or charge because
that was when the client suffered damage. The defendants were in
breach of contract when, at the time of the transfer to the wife or as
soon as practicable thereafter, they failed to take the necessary steps to
protect the plaintiff's interest but since that breach had occurred more
than six years before the issue of the writ, the plaintiff's action in
contract was time-barred. Furthermore the plaintiff had suffered
damage in tort both at the time when the defendants failed to prepare
the declaration of trust, because he had suffered prejudice in entering
into the transfer without the benefit of the protection of a declaration
of trust, and at the time when they failed to register a caution at the
Land Registry, because although that breach was remediable by the
plaintiff up until the wife's sale of the house remedying it depended

on the plaintiff being aware of the breach, which he was not, but since that damage had also occurred more than six years before the issue of the writ the plaintiff's action in tort was time-barred. The appeal would therefore be dismissed.(see p 126 f g, p 127 j to p 128 b e to j, p 129 b, p 132 j to p 133 e, p 134 b c g j and p 136 b c e, post) *Baker* v *Ollard & Bentley(a firm)* (1982) 126 SJ 593 and *DW Moore & Co Ltd* v *Ferrier* [1988] 1 All ER 400 applied. *Midland Bank Trust Co Ltd* v *Hett Stubbs & Kemp (a firm)* [1978] 3 All ER 571 not followed."

Second, a contrasting example from two private commercial reports: the Court of Appeal decision in *Mortgage Express Ltd* v *S. Newman & Co (A firm)* was reported as follows in *Lloyds' Reports Professional Negligence.*[21]

"Solicitors – Indemnity – Solicitors' Indemnity Rules 1993, rule 14(f) – Solicitors' Indemnity Fund obliged not to give indemnity "in respect of any dishonest or fraudulent act or omission" – Whether solicitor had been dishonest in relation to conveyancing transaction.

In 1990 the sole practitioner of a firm of solicitors (N) acted for the purchaser (S) of the lease of a residential property in relation to the purchase. N also acted for the claimant lenders. The claimant was lending £200,000 towards the total purchase price of £275,000, which price was supported by a professional valuation. S soon defaulted and in 1991 the claimant repossessed the property and sold it for about £83,000.

During the course of the transaction, it came to N's knowledge that the person (L) who was selling the property to S was herself acquiring the property in a back-to-back transaction. In L's purchase of the property, the price was only £110,000.

In 1994 the claimant brought proceedings against N claiming damages for negligence. N denied the allegation, but in the event that she was held to be negligent claimed an indemnity from the Solicitors' Indemnity Fund (SIF). SIF denied its liability to indemnify on the basis of rule 14(f) of the Solicitors' Indemnity Rules, which obliged SIF not to provide an indemnity "in respect of any dishonest or fraudulent act or omission." SIF alleged that N had been dishonest.

In relation to the dispute between N and SIF, following a trial Hart J held that N had not been dishonest and granted a declaration that she was entitled to be indemnified by SIF against any damages or costs awarded against her in the claimant's action. SIF appealed, contending that the judge had reached the conclusion that N had not

---

[21] [2000] Lloyd's P.N. 745.

been dishonest on an incorrect premise as to the explanation for her conduct and that he was bound to find that N had been dishonest.

Held, by CA (ALDOUS, TUCKEY and MANCE LJJ), allowing the appeal, that:

1   In relation to the correct approach to the issue of honesty, the relevant factors included the mind of the person responsible, the understanding and practice of solicitors at the relevant time, and the events which took place. Once the facts in relation to these matters had been found, the judge had to decide, according to the standards of right-thinking members of society, whether the act or omission was due merely to incompetence or to dishonesty. That was essentially a question of fact (see para 40).
    –   *Derry* v *Peek* (1889) 14 App Cas 337: *R* v *Ghosh* [1982] QB 1053; *Agip (Africa) Ltd* v *Jackson* [1990] 1 Ch 265; *Royal Brunei Airlines Sdn Bhd* v *Tan* [1995] 2 AC 378; *Heinl* v *Jske Bank (Gibraltar) Ltd* [1999] Lloyds Rep Bank 511; *Twinsectra Limited* v *Yardley* [2000] Lloyds Rep PN 239 considered.
2   In reaching his conclusion that N had not been dishonest, the judge had erred in his reliance on the instructions given to N by the mortgage broker who introduced the transaction to her. There was no reference to the instructions in the terms cited by the judge in the statements of case or the evidence and no reference was made to the point at trial. Accordingly the order could not stand. (see para 34).
3   However, it would be wrong for the Court of Appeal to conclude that N had been dishonest when the trial judge had reached the conclusion that she was not after seeing her cross-examined for one and a half days. It did not follow that, if he had not had the view which he had taken of the mortgage broker's instructions, he would have concluded that N had been dishonest. Accordingly, given that a conclusion as to whether N had acted honestly could only be reached after seeing N give her evidence, a new trial was necessary before another judge (see paras 37 and 38)."

and in this way in *Professional Negligence and Liability Reports*:[22]

"*Solicitor – indemnity by Solicitors Indemnity Fund – whether acts or omissions amount to dishonesty or fraud*

---

[22] [2001] PNLR 5 @ 86.

In a Part 20 claim by N, a solicitor, against the Solicitors Indemnity Fund ("SIF"), SIF declined to grant her indemnity against her loss arising from the Mortgage Express claim, pursuant to rule 14(f) of the Solicitors Indemnity Rules 1993, on the ground that N's acts or omissions amounted to dishonesty or fraud.

In 1990 N, the solicitor, acted for both the purchaser/mortgagor, S, and Mortgage Express, the mortgagee on the purchase of a property by S. The purchase price was £275,000 and the mortgage advance £200,000. N was asked to act for S by B, a mortgage broker. By reason of her absence on holiday and delegation of work, the report on title by N to Mortgage Express apparently was signed on April 17, which stated the date of exchange of contracts was April 12. This was clearly wrong since it was not intended to exchange contracts before completion on or after April 24. By April 25 N was under pressure from B to ensure completion took place forthwith. On her return from holiday N was requested to act for L, the vendor to S, in her purchase transaction which was not yet completed. On April 26 she discovered that the purchase price on L's property was £110,000 and saw documents indicative of a number of shorthold tenancies affecting the property. After consulting the Law Society Ethics and Guidance Department for advice, N agreed to and did act for L. She visited the property to establish that it was vacant. By this stage she had received the £200,000 advance from Mortgage Express. On April 26 she received a banker's draft from S to complete the matter. On April 27 N proceeded to complete the transactions because she did not believe she should advice S about the wisdom of the transaction or to advise Mortgage Express because she stated she believed that if they were comfortable with the valuation, she need do no more than ensure a good title on vacant possession. Then N transferred the balance owing on L's purchase, some £103,000, to L's vendor and then completed the purchase by S from L. N registered S as proprietor of the leasehold title and Mortgage Express as first legal chargee. In fact, the true value of the property at the time was no more than £150,000. After the purchase few payments were made under the Mortgage and in 1992 the property was sold, realising £83,000.

At trial before Hart J., it was SIF's case that in all the circumstances N had wilfully shut her eyes to the obvious, or wilfully and recklessly failed to make enquiries which an honest and reasonable solicitor would have made, that this amounted to dishonesty, and therefore they were entitled to refuse indemnity under rule 14(f). The judge, however, gave judgment for the solicitor. He made certain findings in the solicitor's favour, in particular that N had been told by B at the outset of the transaction that B was not the kind of client who required to be advised of detailed matters in respect of the transaction, that B "was happy with the valuation" and N's "retainer need not extend to doing more than the bare minimum in the way of mechanical conveyancing."

SIF appealed and argued that this factual finding was not open to the judge because it was contrary to N's pleaded case and not consistent with her witness statement or her evidence at the trial. N's counsel conceded that there was evidence upon which the judge could have found that B so instructed N, but the decision could be upheld on the wider ground that she did suspect a mortgage fraud.

Held, allowing the appeal and ordering a retrial:

1   where honesty was in issue the essential duty of the judge was to decide, according to the standard of right-thinking members of society, whether the act or omission was due merely to incompetence or to dishonesty.
2   In doing so, the judge must make findings based on and consistent with the party's pleaded case and the evidence;
3   Here the basis on which the judge had found that the solicitor had not been dishonest was flawed and it was only possible to conclude whether the solicitor was dishonest or not by a judge seeing and hearing the witness. There was no alternative but to order a retrial."

The obvious differences in style and contents suggest that the reliability and personal view of the editorial opinion expressed in the headnote should be a matter of concern to you, or at least something to which you are alive. In specialist reports editors are drawn from the field of practice with which the reports are concerned. Some published reports are associated with particular sets of specialist chambers whose members contribute to editorial work. This is true of housing, construction, companies, insolvency, professional negligence and family law reporting.

The more general, and more frequent reports, particularly in newspapers and journals need to be treated with care, both because of the emphasis placed on the subject matter by 'headlining' the contents, and also by the use of reported rather than direct speech. Frequently the headline given to a report in, for example, the *Times Law Reports* bears little true relation to the detail of the report it refers to. The compression of the facts and parts of the judgment, particularly collegiate judgments, by the use of reported speech, make such reports dangerous to rely on unless no other source is available. You should always draw a distinction between a full report, and what is plainly *a précis* or a note of a judgment, which may not prove authoritative at all when a transcript of the full judgment is considered.

Just like those film bores who like to count mistakes in continuity, so you can count editorial mistakes in law reports if you have the time and inclination. By and large you can be confident that substantive errors in the judgment cannot be touched by the reporter or his editor, and must be referred back to the judge. Even if the transcript looks obviously wrong or does not make sense, the editor may not amend it, and particularly where the judge confirms what still appears ambiguous or difficult. In *Polley* v *Warner Goodman & Street (A Firm)*[23] the word 'fail' in paragraph [18] should logically and contextually be 'succeed' for both the passage and the judgment to make sense. The editors of the law reports were unable to make the change and it remains a good example of such curiosities.

Reporting and editorial errors do creep in. These include mis-citation of authorities, generally due to proof-reading errors of dates and pagination, although such mis-citation can be the fault of the judge. A particular favourite is the inversion of the numerals in the date. Very occasionally the reporter will actually get the name of the judge wrong, or at least misspelt. More often, and perhaps more importantly, the reporter may miss the fact that the judgment contains more than one *ratio* attaching to different aspects of the decision. For example the case may be reported on a substantive point or a point of procedure but in addition be an important authority in respect of the costs argument at the end, or indeed vice-versa. A carelessly drawn headnote can ignore important subsidiary points in the case.

However, when you read the judgment, you will not.

---

[23] [2003] EWCA Civ 1013;[2003] PNLR 784 @ 789 [18] per Clarke LJ.

BIBLIOGRAPHY

BOOKS

Adler & Van Doren *How to Read a Book* (Touchstone/Simon & Schuster, New York 1972)

Jeremy Bentham *Works* ix

Lord Bingham *The Business of Judging: Selected Essays and Speeches* (OUP 2000)

Benjamin Cardozo *Law and Literature* New York 1925

Coke *Inst.Pt.I*

Lord Denning *The Discipline of Law* (Butterworths 1979)

Ronald Dworkin *Taking Rights Seriously* (Duckworths 1977)

Ronald Dworkin *Law's Empire* (Fontana 1986)

Sir Richard Eggleston QC *Evidence Proof and Probability* (Weidenfeld and Nicolson 1978)

Bryan A. Garner *A Dictionary of Modern Legal Usage* (OUP New York 1987)

Bryan A. Garner *Legal Writing in Plain English* (Chicago 2001)

John Gray *Lawyers Latin: A Vade Mecum* (Robert Hale, London 2002)

 Sir Ernest Gowers *The Complete Plain Words* (Penguin 1990)

Holmes *Common Law* (1881)

JSB Handbook on Ethnic Minority Issues October 1995

JSB *Civil Bench Book* August, 2001 edn.

JSB HRA Magistrates Training Guide 2002

JSB *Equal Treatment Bench Book 2004*

A. L Kaufman *Cardozo* (1998)

Simon Lee *Judging Judges* (Faber and Faber 1989)

David Pannick QC *Advocates* (Oxford 1992)

R.A.Posner *Cardozo: a Study in Reputation* (1990)

Salmond *Jurisprudence* 7th edn. (P&MI) 187

A.H.Smith *Glanville Williams: Learning the Law* 12th edn. (Sweet & Maxwell 2002)

Wambaugh *Study of Cases* 2nd edn (1894)

Lord Wright *Legal Essays and Addresses* 1939

Fox M. & Bell C. *Learning Legal Skills* 3rd edn. Blackstone 1999

Holland J.A.& Webb J.S. *Learning Legal Rules* 5th edn. (OUP 2003)

ARTICLES

Law Reporting and the Amending Hand (1970) NLJ 423 (edit.).

Notes (1970) 86 LQR 299 (edit.)

Peter Aldridge *Precedent in the Court of Appeal – Another View* (1984) 47 MLR 187

C.K.Allen *Precedent and Logic* (1925) CLXIII LQR 332

HH Judge Peter Clark *Telling them Why they've Won or Lost (2001) 8 Tribunals Journal 11*

Gary Edmond *Judicial Representation of Scientific Evidence* (2000) 63 MLR 216

Lord Edmund-Davies *Judicial Activism* (1975) 28 CLP 1

M.D.A. Freeman *Standards of Adjudication, Judicial Law-making and Prospective Overruling* (1973) 26 CLP 166

R.D.Friedman *On Cardozo and Reputation: Legendary Judge, Underrated Justice?* (1991) 12 Cardozo LR 1923.

Peter Goodrich *The Role of Linguistics in Legal Analysis* (1984) 47 MLR 523

Prof. B.V. Harris *Final Appellate Courts Overruling Their Own 'Wrong' Precedents: The Ongoing Search For Principle* (2002) LQR 408

Howard Levinson *The Written Decisions of Social Security Commissioners* (2000) 7 Tribunals Journal 16

Dennis Lloyd *Reason and Logic in the Common Law* (1948) 64 LQR 468

Prof H.K.Lücke *The Common Law: Judicial Impartiality and Judge-Made Law* (1982) 98 LQR 29

Paul Magrath *135 Years of Law Reporting for England and Wales* (ICLR Sept 2001)

Justice Beverley McLachlin *The Role of Judges in Modern Commonwealth Society* (1994) 110 LQR 260

Prof. Basil Markesinis *A Matter of Style* (1994) 110 LQR 607

David Pannick QC *A Note on Dworkin and Precedent* (1980) 43 MLR 36

The Form and Language of Judicial Opinions (2002) 118 LQR 226 by Lord Rodger of Earlsferry

Sir John Salmond *The Superiority of Written Evidence* (1890) 6 LQR XXI 75

Prof Peter Stein, *Elegance in Law* (1961) 77 LQR 242

Decision Drafting – Brief, Balanced and to the Point Martin Wood (2001) 8 Tribunals Journal 2

Weighing the Evidence Mullan and Wilton (2001) 9 Tribunals Journal 2

WEBSITES

www.jsboard.co.uk

www.parliament.uk.

www.parliament.uk/documents/uploadHofLBpJUdicial.pdf

www.tribunals-review.org.uk

LECTURES

Lord Bingham *The Discretion of the Judge* 1990 Royal Bank of Scotland Lecture, Oxford University, 17 May 1990, (reported in [1990] *Denning Law Journal* 27)

Lord Bingham LCJ Address delivered at Westminster Abbey on 17 June 1999 at the Service of Thanksgiving for the Rt. Hon Lord Denning O.M.

Sir John Donaldson M.R.(Chairman) *Judicial Techniques in Arbitration and Litigation* Chartered Institute of Arbitrators, December 1988

HH Judge Marr-Johnson *Giving Judgment* JSB County Court Induction Course, September, 1998

Lord Justice Scott *Judgments and the Role of Judge in the County Court* JSB County Court Induction Course, April, 1992

Sir Christopher Staughton *What's Wrong With the Law in the Year 2000* Inner Temple Millennium Lecture, Inner Temple Hall 29 November 2000

INDEX

ALSO OF INTEREST FROM XPL

Written Advocacy

Andrew Goodman, Barrister, 1 Serjeants Inn

The requirement to produce skeleton arguments has been with us for 10 years, but written advocacy remains in its infancy. Court of Appeal judges admit that cases are decided before oral argument on the strength of written advocacy. Throughout the civil justice system under the CPR the skill is vital – cases are won on lost on the advocate's skill writing, not addressing the court orally. This book provides practical advice in drafting model form pre-action protocol letters of claim; *inter partes* correspondence; Part 36 Offers; skeleton arguments; written opening notes for trial; closing submissions; costs submissions; and much more. Leading practitioners have offered their assistance in producing a book of real authority.

ISBN 1 85811 358 X

Civil Evidence for Practitioners

Dr Joseph Jacob, London School of Economics, Previous Editions Professor Peter Hibbert

The third edition comes at a time when three key developments have placed evidence ever firmly at the heart of successful litigation: the CPR and case management mean ever more emphasis on avoiding waste of costs – in turn meaning that practitioners must focus clearly on the evidence that is necessary for the case and no more, as well as its weight The advent of conditional fee agreements means accurate assessment of the risks inherent in bringing a case becomes of paramount importance to the financial success of the lawyer. *Civil Evidence for Practitioners* is unique among works of evidence - it is practical, readable and authoritative.

ISBN 1 85811 314 8

To order:

**xpl publishing, 99 hatfield road, st albans, AL1 4JL
tel 0870 143 2569   fax 0845 456 6385
web: www.xplpublishing.com**

● dpe@email.com

Printed in the United Kingdom
by Lightning Source UK Ltd.
108983UKS00001B/79-120